What HIT me? Living w

A guide to diagnosis

A patient'_ ,

by

Genny Masterman

Disclaimer

All material in this book is provided for your information only and may not be construed as medical advice or instruction. No action or inaction should be taken based solely on the contents of this information; instead, readers should consult appropriate health professionals on any matter relating to their health and well-being.

The information and opinions expressed here are believed to be accurate, based on the best judgement available to the author, and readers who fail to consult with appropriate health authorities assume the risk of any injuries. In addition, the information and opinions expressed here do not necessarily reflect the views of every contributor to the book. The author acknowledges occasional differences in opinion and welcomes the exchange of different viewpoints. The publisher is not responsible for errors or omissions.

Readers interested in sending their suggestions, ideas or complaints can do so via e-mail at info@histamineintolerance.org.uk. This book is part of the Histamine Intolerance Awareness project, supported by a growing number of volunteers.

Layout: www.panthera.cc

"What is food to one may be fierce poison to others."

Lucretius

CONTENTS

1. THANKS

I owe a lot of thanks to a lot people by now and if I have left anyone out I profusely apologise in advance. Some of you have been extremely patient with me and also kind. Mum, what would I be without you! Have a look at the fridge magnet. You are the best of all mums in the entire universe. Special thanks also to my family, especially Rene, Susi & Merlin, Marcel & Dorry, Marga, webmaster James, Barbara & Dad, Paul and Fran, to name but a few.

Many, many thanks for your individual ways of supporting me to Leo Mazakarini, who was my mentor for actually writing a book and without whom I could never have done this. Prim. Univ. Doz. Dr. A. Thomas Endler, Univ. –Doz. Prim. DI. DDr. Hans Schön, Prof. Thomas Bieber, Ph.D. Natalija Novak and Dr Ralph Bauer at the University of Bonn, Ing. Mag. Dr. Fabian Kanz at the Medical University of Vienna, Dr Ken Fleming, Dr. Hassan Abdulrazzak, Mag Helmuth Schmutz, Angelika Widhalm, President of patient support group FruLak&Co in Vienna and her team, Dr Susanne Feigl, Pamela T., Sabine Geyr, Sylvia Obenauer, Michael Zechmann of the NMI Portal (Portal for adverse reactions to food), Allergy UK's Muriel Simmons, and Lindsey Mc Manus as well as John Collard, Ronke Shona the incredibly supportive food scientist who is one of the kindest people I have ever met and has endured many hours of virulent discussion with me, Andrea König of the Mastocytosis Initiative and dietician Cornelia Boboschewski-Sos. Further there are butchers Wally Dutton & his crew at Duttons Butchers, Keith at Rose Farm, Kay and all involved at Winsors Farm shop, the wonderful Diana Mather, Rex Bloomstein, Joe Barth, Mike Wadding, Jonathan & Selina, Sarah Green, Mark Sangster, the many Pauls around me, Steven R., Hywel W., Jon A., Charles O. and the Northern Advantage Team, Leigh Wharton, Dan Hartenstein (you rock, mate), Susan & Helmut Katzmann, Andi Link, Renate Wiener and my closest friends Gerald Wiener and Andi Komenda.

Last but not least there all the members of the Facebook group, the supporters of the Facebook page, those who helped set up and run the histamineintolerance.org.uk website and talked me into writing a blog, the patients, who have written to me via the histamineintolerance.org.uk website and those who have signed the petition, all of whom shall remain anonymous. This is for you, written with the best of intentions.

2. INTRODUCTION

I shall best begin by telling my story and how I came to the idea of writing this book in the hope of giving others, who might be in the same situation, a chance of regaining some quality in their lives.

It was one of the most beautiful summers that I had ever experienced in the city of Vienna. This is where I grew up and go back to, to visit my friends and my father. I have lived there most of my life although my family originally comes from the UK and The Netherlands. It needs to be said that I am normally a very positive person, full of energy, who shrugs off minor ailments. So although some of this chapter might read like one long moan – that's not how I am. But I have to spell it out in order for you to understand it – so here goes.

I had been feeling a little queasy, to say the least, for quite a while. Only a few weeks earlier, while still in the UK, I had a problem with one of my teeth, an infection, and was given an antibiotic –later in my voyage of discovery I was to learn that this antibiotic contains one of the very substances I should not have taken in combination with all my other health issues. The barrel was full already and this medication caused the barrel to overflow and sparked off a very severe reaction.

A year earlier I had started feeling increasingly tired and occasionally suffered from the "trots", to put it politely. In addition I was increasingly plagued by cramps in my abdomen. And since this was not happening on a regular basis I played it all down, as one does. My psoriasis, which I have had ever since I can think, started to play up really badly. The previous year I was plagued by a bout of what may have been urticaria – it was nasty whatever it was - which went away again after a few months. No cream I smeared on the red patches seemed to help. The irritating circles just mysteriously disappeared from one week to the next. At the time I did not know what it was, and only during my research during the writing of this book I have found out what it actually could have been. For several years my legs were swelling up in summer. My eyes were full of gunge in the morning; I blamed the contacts but still kept wearing them out of pure vanity. Before midday I could set the clock by regular sneezing fits after breakfast. I blamed some mystery plants which, according to this particular theory of mine, would have had to release pollen all year round. I also developed a tremor in my early twenties, and was often asked why I was so nervous that I was shaking - even when I felt perfectly calm. When

I got annoyed about it I started shaking even more. It seemed like a lose-lose situation, especially when my head felt like it was going to bob off my shoulders when the shake would take over the rest of my body, especially in exam and stress situations. The list of symptoms and occasions is long, and I always had some self-diagnosable explanation for everything.

My speculation was that possibly I just needed some rest because I might have been too stressed, and the pains were because I might be getting my period, although it often didn't start, and the trots because I might have eaten something that had gone bad because maybe I had been sold something that was well past its use-by date, or similar... . Are you confused? I was!

I guess I was not so wrong with the whole 'out of date' idea in a way, but that is as far as I got. Now I know that cured meats and mature cheeses, some of my favourite former foods contain high levels of histamine, not because they have 'gone bad' but due to the way they are matured. I am now continuing to reintroduce them carefully and one by one, in order to test my personal threshold,

So, in Vienna in the midst of all that lovely warmth, while spending the evenings next to open French windows with friends, drinking red wine and eating lovely dishes, mostly with tomatoes in them, and happily working away on a project for a client by day, it all went pear-shaped. The cramps got worse, I got desperately tired. On top of that I felt sick, or rather bloated, in my abdomen. "Ah, it's a bug!" I thought. Going to the doctor did not cross my mind. I felt I had no time for that anyway, as usual. I held out until about the fourth week, when I decided that it might be something more serious than just a bug after all and that maybe I should listen to my friends and go to the doctor.

Sitting in front of him, I told him of my dilemma - that I had to continue to work because I am freelance and must keep clients happy or else I fear I might not get a good reference, which is what is vital to my career. You're only as good as your last job. I work as an Associate Producer and Fixer, mainly on television documentaries. It is a tough job that involves a lot of pressure, with long and stressful days, but is still very rewarding. You really need to be fit for this job otherwise you won't last too long in the industry. I had not seen this particular medic for a long time because I had moved to the UK a couple of years earlier. But he had the broadest knowledge of my medical history. In general I always went to doctors wherever I happened to be in the world, so my data is certainly spread around. I told him about the last year, that I had been to doctors several times because of various cramps in my lower abdomen, but they had never found anything and put it all down to stress or something similar. What they all agreed on was that absolutely "nothing was wrong with me"! I was truly confused by all of this, because by now I was convinced that there was something really weird going on. Had I turned into a classic hypochondriac?

The doctor listened patiently. First of all he gave me a good old Viennese-style, but still friendly, telling off. I should have been sitting in front of him four weeks ago when it started. Diarrhoea is nothing to be messed with. He suggested we do some tests. One of them would be for an enzyme called diamine oxidase. At my request he explained what it was and why he did the test, but it all went right in one ear and out the other. I was too exhausted to take anything in.

A couple of days later it turned from bad to worse. My body reacted badly to anything I ate or even drank. I was dehydrating really fast, and we were in the middle of the hot phase with my clients. I did actually tell my clients that there was a small problem, and promised to keep someone else in the background as back-up in case I or my clients felt that I was unable to work on the project according to the expected standards or put myself in any danger. I muttered vaguely about a "grumbling appendix".

I checked with the doctor, and he gave me advice on what I should do – basically to go home and look after myself. Finally I was presented with the facts. I had very low levels of the enzyme diamine oxidase. The result was that I suffered from Histamine Intolerance (HIT). I was to avoid tomatoes, aubergines, spinach, cured meats, mature cheeses, and most of all my beloved red wine. Information pack in hand, I went back to base, and shortly after, home to the UK. At last – my condition had a name!

The list of foods to avoid or reduce for a while was long – very long. At first glance I felt there was nothing left to eat. The list of "forbidden foods" was basically all those things that had been on my plate on a daily basis. I was gripped by panic. But it was the beginning of a new life, a wonderful life full of energy and, most importantly, without pain.

When I returned home the first thing I tried to do was to find a dietician who could help me to work out a plan. I felt like a fish out of water, I needed help. Getting an appointment took an endless amount of time, and meanwhile I resorted to German sources on the internet. I bought German literature on the subject. All that I could get from English language websites was fuzzy, scatty and often in medical terminology quite foreign to me. The dietician I finally was able to meet in a hospital was sweet, sympathetic and helpful, and even though I was admittedly her first patient with this condition she had never heard of before, she actually gave me some great advice on how to go about it all. She did what she could with the means she had, after I, the patient, explained to her what I had read up about this intolerance. By that time I had already started to explain to everybody else around me what this was, so I was pretty good at it by now.

The diet seemed to work - kind of. Four weeks further down the line things were quite a lot better. I started to go on a really "healthy" diet, tried to learn more about the 5-a-day principle, and learned to cook. But something wasn't quite right. I kept on getting really nasty bouts of wind and diarrhoea, sudden, painful, that sometimes even had me lying on the floor, as I had in the past, gasping for breath. I just couldn't figure it out, even when I was really good and cut out the alcohol altogether - which I was not always very disciplined about.

On my next trip to Vienna I went to visit my father once more. We were watching TV, his wife had just made a low-histamine dinner for me, when an item about an HIT patient was broadcast on Austrian TV. She explained about the HIT condition and the two other intolerances she has on top of that, and how she selects her food in the supermarket. I decided to track her down. Through her I was able to contact several HIT patients who are members of a self-help group. All of them urged me to get some more tests done, since they did not know anyone who just had histamine intolerance alone. The stories of their particular search for the truth behind their symptoms were truly mind-blowing.

So I went back to the UK and contacted the GP. Of course I had to explain what it was about all over again because I got to see a different GP from last time. But things were going so slowly through the system that by the time I went to Vienna again I still had no answer. Not much time was wasted in deciding to go back to the Austrian medic. I must add at this point that when I went for these tests I was in full denial. The prospect of having to combine two diets with two very long lists of foods to avoid was gruelling, unthinkable and felt a bit like a "well you might just as well stop living then" kind of life sentence. I vividly remember saying "I am sure that I don't have any of these, but I just want to check, and prove everyone wrong", and putting on my brave smile.

I had tests done for gluten, lactose, fructose and a long list of allergies. All of them were negative – except for one. Guess what - I also happen to have dietary fructose malabsorption. Surprise, surprise. And guess what again ... with this tweak I have been able to control the symptoms, although it was all terribly complicated at the beginning. So here's to everyone in Vienna, "Thank you! Thank you! Thank you!"

Within only six months I learned to cook all kinds of different meals which would not even have crossed my mind before. I have learned to experiment, pick different meals and adapt them. My threshold has risen to a certain extent and if I am lucky then the diamine oxidase levels will be normal again sometime in the future. But who knows when or if. For all I know I will just have to live with it.

Over time I realised that there are only a very few medical professionals who are even aware of the existence of this intolerance. The situation may not be perfect in continental Europe, but I can confirm that at least it has reached public awareness in the German language area to some degree. At least every second person I talk to there has grasped the general concept, and I have even met people on my travels that have been diagnosed. Some pharmacies will immediately pull up their information on their computer and give you advice on what you should or should not be able to take.

Being the daughter of two former war correspondents and myself having taken the route of working in the world of television documentaries, I dropped myself quite deliberately into a flurry of research to try and find out what the deal is. The deal looks distinctly rotten for those who are affected by the condition. No matter where they are in the world, most HITers are struggling with their diet, do not know what medication to take or not to take, have no idea if their reaction is because of HIT or something else. Many are diagnosed and left to their own devices once their pockets have been emptied. My question is, how can this be in what we call the modern age? Aren't we supposed to be a little more advanced than this?

Concerning the number of people currently affected, there are several estimates swirling around. Personally I don't care about an exact number or statistic of people who are out there struggling with this rather elusive intolerance. It doesn't matter anymore if it is thousands or millions. We are not a number but individuals, each of us with a life, family and friends.

The main objective is that help becomes available for those who have this condition, for whatever reason. I do understand that since the diet really is the key, and there is not much to sell here, there is little interest in research. I also understand that the media still needs some more proof of its genuineness and significance, and that, at the time of writing this book, this may still be considered to be something we might call a "niche subject" = less interesting because of limited reader, listener or viewer numbers. I fully comprehend that at least some in the pharmaceutical industry do not have any interest in pursuing any further research because some of their products will certainly be branded unsuitable for a lot of their consumers once the research is confirmed, hence less profit. I also understand that there may not be much participation from a lot of food manufactures, since the prospect of having to admit that certain meals consist of chemical brews and are actually not suitable for a percentage of the population, and in the case of someone with HIT can even be a cause of death from anaphylactic shock, is certainly not what they are aiming for.

BUT:

It is absolute priority that this subject is being properly discussed out in the open, and there is a proper system in place in hospitals, at GP's practices, dieticians offices, dentists, the lot, for those who have this condition. Those who have HIT should be equipped with a pass similar to those for diabetics, and should not be turned away at hospitals and told to 'sleep it off', just because hospitals may not know what to do with them. This is one more of the rather bizarre and forgettable experiences I have had in the last two years – and apparently from what I hear I am not the only one who has experienced problems at a hospital... . I was able to deal with it in the end, but I was reeling with anger after having to cope with a nasty infection. Not exactly the best for an HITer's histamine count either, which automatically goes up when a person is stressed. If hospital staff had the relevant education, training and the information then this would not happen in the first place.

The following chapters are based on peer-reviewed and published research conducted by scientists and researchers all over the world. References can be found in the back of this book. Whatever conclusion you may come to after reading these chapters, if you think you might be a candidate for histamine intolerance then I strongly advise you to consult with a GP or nutritionist about a diet. It would be even better if you could get yourself referred to a professional who has a grounded knowledge of allergies and intolerances. Do make sure that any people offering medical advice outside the NHS or any other state-sponsored system are registered practitioners. In the UK, for example, that would be with the General Medical Council (GMC), where you can check whether the doctor you plan to visit actually has a license to practice (further information on the GMC website www.gmc-uk.org). Self-proclaimed experts or so-called world-experts, especially on the internet, are to be regarded with extreme caution, and should be checked thoroughly in advance before you put your life in their hands.

If you do decide to go on this diet then I have included some recipes in the second part of the book. These are recipes that I have either worked out and tested myself or have been supplied by friends. They are food for ideas and need to be chosen according to the person's degree of intolerance in combination with any other conditions. This means that not all recipes will be suitable for everyone. All in all, do not be afraid of trying out new versions, adapting old recipes you may once have liked. There is a lot you can do.

So here we go: Experiment! Experiment! Experiment!

3. HISTAMINE INTOLERANCE – IN A NUTSHELL

Knowledge is power. Some of you may find this chapter really hard going, but I urge you to persist. Others will devour the knowledge, learning at last what is behind it all. The other reason for putting all this information here is that you can take it and rub it under the noses of those who just don't believe that HIT exists. Friends and family, doctors and dieticians, may need a bit of convincing. It also contains information you can refer back to if something is not clear in a later chapter, or in something else you are reading on the subject. But don't worry. Plough through this and it gets easier, more down to earth and more personal. I promise.

What is histamine?

In chemical terms, histamine is one of a group of biogenic amines. It's a fellow that has its fingers in all pies. Let's talk about the positives first: it helps us as neurotransmitter sending messages throughout the body, contributes to the regulation of body temperatures and to our memory. It also helps us with the wound-healing process, has functional roles in connection with allergies, in our stomach, in the brain and even in our blood cells. It even plays an important part in the development of embryos. All in all it is quite an all-rounder and a very essential piece of our kit.

What is Histamine Intolerance?

Histamine Intolerance (HIT), also called enteral histaminosis, is a condition that is caused by the lack or reduced activity of an enzyme called diamine oxidase (DAO). A lot of DAO is produced in the intestinal mucosa, the membrane that lines your guts, and is generally responsible for metabolising (breaking down or processing) histamine that enters our bodies in the form of foods and drinks. Amongst those foods which have been classified as having higher levels of histamine are tomatoes, spinach, aubergines, avocado, pickles, cured meats, mature cheeses and yeast. There are also other foods, such as some citrus fruits and strawberries, which are believed to release the histamine already stored in blood and mast cells. Certain additives in foods and drinks, such as glutamate, food colourings and sulphites, for example, are believed to have the same effect. The subject of food and histamine will be looked at more closely in the following chapters. There is also another enzyme by the name of histamine-N-methyltransferase, to be found in the human tissue, which currently takes a bit of a back seat in discussions, although it should not be ignored! Patients, who are taking medication which blocks this enzyme should consult with their doctor about possibly changing to another more suitable medication.

What is diamine oxidase ?

DAO is responsible for metabolising – thus breaking down – histamine, and also other biogenic amines - the close relatives of histamine, so to speak. (These other biogenic amines also play an important role in the way our body functions. Some act as neurotransmitters or tissue hormones, some are found when something decomposes. A selection of these biogenic amines is tyramine, dopamine, noradrenaline, tryptamine and cadaverine. Tyramine, for example, is also found in red wine. Cadaverine is a bacterial product which we can smell when animal tissue is decomposing.)

You have to see DAO as being like a regiment of little security guards most of whom are ready and waiting to intercept an advancing mass of histamines and/or their relatives. When too big a crowd of histamines arrive, then the DAO guards might be overwhelmed, either because they have been outnumbered, or because they are wrestling with histamine's brothers and sisters, or they might have been sedated by an outsider, often by slipping them a dose of a specific medication. The histamines are then free to rampage through your digestive and the rest of your system and can at some point reach a toxic level. Parallels with an uncontrolled crowd entering a football stadium come to mind.

What can trigger histamine intolerance?

Now, DAOs are very sensitive little things and do need some tender loving care because otherwise they will not function correctly. There are several reasons why this enzyme can be negatively affected:

- There has been an intestinal infection and the production of the enzyme is disturbed, or the cells in the small intestine do not have a sufficient amount of DAO present in them.

- DAO production is affected because of another intolerance that affects the digestive system (see other intolerances). Not exclusively, but quite often this is when the patient's symptoms include diarrhoea.

- DAO is blocked or suppressed and its function is impaired. For example, let's say, if a patient with HIT is given a specific medication, such as certain antibiotics that suppress DAO, the result could be that symptoms get more severe because histamine is then able to build up in the system to an uncomfortable level. Other blockers are hidden in specific foods and additives.

- Other foods, food additives or medications may have a histamine-releasing effect. Just one example is morphine, used in anaesthetics, also for surgery. A person who is unable to degrade the released histamine and who then adds more through food will certainly feel the effects and can be at risk in hospital.

- Other biogenic amines, such as tyramine, putrescine, spermine and cadaverine, also need the DAO enzyme in order to be broken down. This can also cause a temporary DAO shortage. There's just not enough to go around.

- Alcohol is an arch-enemy of our DAO friends. It releases histamine that is already stored in the body cells, then uses one of its by-products called acetaldehyde to suppress the DAO enzyme. This also enhances the effect of other biogenic amines, histamine's close relatives, who happen to pass through at the same time.

- In some very rare cases, it appears, people have been born with DAO deficiency.

- In the case of an additional genuine allergy the body itself starts to release extra histamine. If foods with a high amount of histamine are eaten at this stage, then it is possible for the amount of histamine in the body to reach toxic levels.

There are several mechanisms normally at work in our bodies that stop an excessive amount of histamine from entering the bloodstream. But if these mechanisms fail because of the reasons above then the person concerned can be facing some very unpleasant consequences. The severity depends on the individual threshold.

Food poisoning and HIT

The best-known example of a histamine "overdose" is food poisoning from fish, where high histamine levels are often at least a partial contributor to severe illness, especially after consuming warm water fish such as tuna. This can affect anyone, however. When two people have exactly the same meal, a person with a low histamine threshold can be severely ill while a healthy person may only feel slightly off-colour. Several rules and regulations have been established by the European Union in order to prevent fish products with high histamine levels from landing on our plates. One of these regulations limits the amount of histamine that fish is allowed to contain when it reaches the consumer.

Pre-prepared foods and HIT

HIT patients need to be aware of the dangers lurking for them in pre-prepared food. A whole industry nowadays is based on the processing of food, from frozen meals to canned or packaged soup. These widely available products come in all shapes and sizes and have often become a great asset for our society. We all, in some way, have become dependent on the industry, whether economically or just to save time. But this 20th Century development also has its drawbacks and these have only become visible recently. Some of us are simply not able to digest some of the chemicals used as preservatives and taste-enhancers. Even without these, some 'normal' ingredients can trip us up if the labelling is unclear. This can turn the mere consumption of a ready-meal into a journey into hell for those who react more severely. It does not mean there is anything inherently wrong with the product – it is just wrong for us! The laws of chemistry determine that a certain build-up of chemicals will at some point spark a reaction, also in our bodies, especially when our diets are very simple and we keep eating the same food regularly. This could explain why we suddenly react especially badly to precisely those foods and products we like most. The convenience game turns against us.

Pre-prepared foods have thus become identified as one of the highest ranking culprits with regard to HIT because some of them have extremely high histamine content. More of the reasons why will be explained as you read on. The only positive way out is for the food industry to realise the economic potential of food intolerance and depends on its willingness to cooperate with us, the consumers. They have proved that they can do it, with "free-from" ranges for some conditions. We HIT folk are a big and growing market segment. Together, we can be strong! As a great friend and supporter of mine said, "Our bodies should not have to cater for the food industry, but the food industry for our bodies!"

Wine and HIT

Another example for "overdosing" is red wine. Red wine generally contains high levels of histamine, which is why some people suffer from symptoms when they have had only one glass. One of the most well known and very obvious reactions is flushing in the cheeks or red patches on the chest. This is not to be confused with wine allergy, where symptoms appear much faster as a reaction to one or more of the components in the wine. In general a bad reaction to wine, though, does not necessarily have to mean an automatic histamine intolerance since the affected person may actually have an intolerance, or even an allergy, to another component in this particular beverage. This means red wine may be a strong indicator of histamine intolerance, but is not a means of self-diagnosis.

Why do some of us get HIT?

Histamine intolerance appears to be a condition that is acquired over time. Some experts are, however, exploring the theory that there is a sub-group of HIT sufferers who are genetically pre-disposed to being affected by HIT. Scientists examining this are trying to find out whether there is a common genetic denominator in this sub-group which is also affected by other adverse reactions to food, such as celiac disease, Morbus Crohn and other similar digestive disorders. It will be down to scientists to get to the bottom of what the basic causes are for a person acquiring it. The current generally accepted hypothesis, though, is that this may be a life-style related issue. Basically our bodies are not given the time to adapt to a fast-changing world. Seeing as how our digestive systems have not changed much since the Stone Age, it is remarkable how resilient they are to what we throw at them.

HIT mimics allergy and vice versa

The main problem with trying to define HIT as a cause of discomfort is that, first and foremost, it mimics the symptoms of an allergy. It does this so well that most doctors initially think the symptoms are caused by an allergy. They can be taken in just as easily as someone can be taken in by the double of a well-known person in the street. The symptom caused by an allergic reaction might be asthma; the symptom caused by histamine intolerance might be... have a guess... asthma. Histamine intolerance is very frequently confused with allergies. Excluding the possibility of allergy as a responsible culprit is extremely important, and should be one of the first things you should check out. HIT is also frequently "diagnosed" as IBS, which can be another way of saying "I know you've got something, but I don't know what it is, so deal with it." This response by people who have no knowledge of this condition is understandable because histamine plays the major role in allergies. If you have an allergy, such as hay-fever, then you take anti-histamine tablets, don't you? The words 'allergy' and 'histamine' are linked in most peoples' minds, and for a good reason too.

This brings in the subject of the role of allergologists in the discipline of recognising the difference between the two. Future allergologists (who study the medical side of allergies) are well-versed in recognising signs and identifying the cause of histamine-related reactions. An integration of HIT into their field of expertise can only bring them more recognition by patients as well as an upgrade in reputation. Some allergologists have already realised this and are at the forefront of this new development. Much is being discussed about them on the web, which almost certainly puts them in a very good position, at least in the public eye.

One of the organisations that has now integrated food intolerances and HIT into their program is the charity Allergy UK, which has a dedicated team of experts, including gastroenterologists and nutritionists, now working on this very issue. Their services include a dedicated website, a separate forum section for food intolerances, an on-line helpline as well as a telephone helpline. A highly encouraging development to say the least.

The difference between HIT and allergy

But allergies and HIT are completely different, and they can both show up in different ways. In the case of allergies, histamine is released by the body as part of an excessive immune system response to a normally harmless substance like pollen or peanuts. Cross-reactivity in people who are allergic to certain pollens or other substances also plays a role. On the other hand, in the case of HIT the immune system is not involved at all. It is more the fact that our old friend DAO is not doing its job properly, for whatever reason. Another major difference is that symptoms will be felt almost instantaneously in allergies and in severe cases can result in an instant anaphylactic shock even when the person is only exposed to a trace of the culprit substance – remember the horror stories about traces of peanut, resulting in the 'may contain nuts' labels on packaging, or mention of the fact that something has been produced in a factory where nuts might just have been some time in history....

With HIT it is also possible to experience an anaphylactic shock, but it takes much longer to build up to that stage. The symptoms of HIT take much longer to appear, sometimes as long as 24 hours depending on how fast it all passes through our bodies. This also depends on the type of food that has been ingested, how much histamine is in it, how much of the enzyme DAO is available and its level of activity, or in how far it has been suppressed by different factors such as certain medications. This makes it all the harder to identify the 'culprit'.

Symptoms of HIT

The symptoms of HIT might be one or a combination of the following:

Digestive disorders:

Diarrhoea, stomach ache, cramps, feeling nauseous, full, bloated

Diarrhoea alternating with normal motions (Irritable Bowel Syndrome – IBS), chronic gastrointestinal diseases, Morbus Crohn, colitis ulcerosa

Chronic constipation

Flatulence and feeling of fullness, often quite extreme and irrespective of food intake, sometimes already beginning in the morning

Symptoms affecting head and face:

Headaches, similar to migraine, where drugs are often ineffective

Redness and feeling hot around the face and neck

Runny or blocked nose and weepy or red eyes, often during and after meals, although there has been no diagnosis of any allergies

Fits of dizziness, often feeling as though the head is stuffed with cotton wool.

Sleeping disorders, extreme tiredness, often during or after meals, which results in compulsive sleeping disorder and requires several hours of sleep, often without a feeling of recovery (feeling "knocked out")

Sudden psychological changes (e.g. aggressiveness, inattentiveness, lack of concentration), often during or after intake of a meal

Panic attacks

Skin problems:

Skin rashes, eczema, urticaria, partly already existing for a long time, coming and going although there seems to be no identifiable cause

Acne rosacea (chronic facial redness, sometimes with scales and additional pimples)

Wheals

Itchiness

Chest area:

Asthma

Cardiac arrhythmia, such as a fast beating or irregularly heart beat

Women:

Dysmenorrhoea (severe period pains)

HIT symptoms go away during pregnancy and return after birth of child

Other symptoms:

Feeling chilly, shivering, indisposition

Low blood pressure (rarely high blood pressure)

Breaking out in a sweat.

The worst-case scenario can be that a patient suffers an **anaphylactic shock**. In many cases a combination of several symptoms can be seen.

Medical units will face the challenge in future of recognising the indications of HIT, and this will be especially relevant to those experts in the field of gastroenterology and allergy, as well as all other medical fields.

HIT and other health issues

The other problem is that HIT might be one of a combination of health issues from which a person suffers, such as other intolerances, allergies or chemical sensitivities, which is why it is very important to work with professionals to work out the whole picture. HIT often, but not exclusively, appears in combination with:

An allergy to one or several substances

Coeliac disease

Lactose intolerance

Fructose malabsorption or fructose intolerance (rare)

Sorbite intolerance

Casein Intolerance

Glutamate intolerance.

Quite often HIT has been identified as a secondary condition, caused by another health issue such as the conditions above.

HIT testing issues

Because of the limited awareness and lack of education among doctors, despite research results piling up to a point where they cannot be ignored, tests for HIT, developed in Austria and more widely on offer in a number of European countries, are very difficult to obtain. That leaves the sufferer currently with only one option. This is to test for HIT by using a temporary elimination diet. This needs the help of a practitioner who might be open-minded on the subject of intolerances or at least a referral to a dietician. A competent dietician, currently also very scarce in connection with HIT, will work out a balanced diet plan in order to establish which foods are causing trouble. The professionals have to work together with the patient in order to establish how long this temporary elimination diet will have to be maintained, depending on the seriousness of the condition and the number of other health issues involved. Normally an elimination diet does not last longer than 3-4 weeks.

At the time of writing this book it is extremely difficult to get access to this kind of diagnosis in the UK. If you are unable to get a diagnosis please notify your MP and ask them why you are unable to get the service you are requesting.

The speculation over numbers

It is difficult, if not even impossible, to say what percentage of the population suffers from HIT. The lowest estimate given is 1%, the highest 5% in the Western population – though some sources believe it is even higher. It is also difficult to determine at this stage what degrees of HIT affect how many people. If we take the most conservative estimate of 1%, given by an Austrian expert at an institute for allergy and food intolerance who has been studying the subject over a long period of time, this would mean that approximately 600.000 people in the UK, for instance, are affected by HIT to a greater or lesser degree, depending on their individual threshold. That is a great many people considering that only a very few know about it. An estimated 80 percent of those affected are reckoned to be female and they are predominantly aged around 40.

Discussion topics

This gives rise to a whole bunch of questions: Why do so many medics not know anything about it? Is it because there is little funding for research on the subject, or because there is no backing for research from a powerful major company that might see a prospective financial gain - because there is no 'magic bullet'? Have medical professionals got stuck in the rut of scepticism with regard to food intolerances as was prevalent a decade ago? Why have they not moved forward to use fresh scientific knowledge to establish the validity of these adverse reactions to food? Have they not kept track of the scientific evidence that has been produced since then?

How much money is going down the drain at the different health services in each country because people are being treated for the symptoms but not the cause? These health services have huge budgets to provide care for their consumers, us, the patients. Most patients who feel well will certainly not go to the doctor without a very good reason. How much suffering is being caused to patients by this lack of knowledge, or downright ignorance? How many patients are thus being prescribed the wrong medication which, in many cases, makes their condition worse, not better? How can it be that a condition that can be controlled by a change of eating habits and, in theory, does not require any extra medication, has been overlooked and under-diagnosed? That diagnosis is now scientifically possible, after all, either through a simple blood test or an elimination diet. So why is it not generally available?

A big re-think and more patient-friendly approach is desperately needed, unless many of those in the medical profession don't want to redeem their honour and their credibility. We patients are not stupid. We need people who listen to us, not people who tick boxes in order to meet targets. We need doctors who will work with us, not patronise us. Many gods in white have a nasty smudge on that pristine coat and do not look quite so divine and all-knowing to their patients any longer. Along the way they harm the reputation of those colleagues who are doing some fantastic work. So many patients are flocking in desperation to all kinds of alternative medicine, some of which may be good for a partial solution and some of which may result in you being given advice that could be extremely harmful... .

4. HOW DO I FIND OUT IF I HAVE HIT?

Questions to ask yourself

Should you be able to answer two or more of the eight questions below with a yes, then it is a clinical indication that you may be suffering from histamine intolerance. It would then be advisable to take this knowledge to the medical expert you believe is most suitable to help you to obtain a further diagnosis.

1. Do you frequently have headaches or migraines?

2. Are you intolerant (do you get any obvious symptoms) to red wine and other alcoholic beverages?

3. Do you have any bad reactions to mature cheeses, cured meats, tomatoes, ketchup or chocolate?

4. Have you had any stomach or intestinal troubles, especially with soft faeces or diarrhoea over a longer period of time?

5. Have you frequently suffered from low blood pressure?

6. Have you had any heart problems such as a high pulse rate (tachycardia) or heart rhythm disturbances (cardiac arrhythmia)?

7. For women: Do you have severe pain on the first day of your period (dysmenorrhoea)?

8. Do you experience sea sickness or motion sickness?

Where do I find an expert – or finding your way around the labyrinth?

This is unfortunately still a bit of a challenge. Clinical establishments in many places still know little or nothing about HIT. This leaves people affected by HIT to fend for themselves. They remain extremely vulnerable.

There are labs scattered all over the globe that offer tests via the internet. Some, for example, offer to send a test kit to your home, to take to the GP, and then send the sample to a pathology lab close to your home. There is no talk of anamnesis on some of the sites. The cost is sometimes prohibitive and you need to look closely at what form of transport is chosen as well as whether the blood sample is still valid by the time it reaches the lab, depending on packaging, length of transport as well as temperature fluctuations, and whether that particular lab has had much experience with this test in the first place. Some of the companies might be very professional and know what they are doing, but just snooping around the net and selecting anyone at random could easily be compared to putting your money in a slot-machine at the Casino. You may be lucky, but the risk is high, and it is your health that is at stake.

In the UK it is possible for a GP to send the blood sample to a lab that provides services to doctors. This will cost the patient approximately GBP 35,-. This cost is not covered by the NHS (as of 2010). The NHS Customer Service Centre at the Department of Health confirms that "Neither Departmental officials nor the NHS professionals whom we contacted were aware of this test" as of June of that year, and further states that "It is not one that is offered in mainstream NHS Clinical Pathology Accredited laboratories run by appropriately qualified immunologists that provide NHS specialised laboratory diagnostic services for allergy." And further, "It is conceivable that the test might be offered by some private laboratories in the UK, or by laboratories in Europe. As it is not an established NHS-provided test, neither officials nor NHS clinicians are aware of any information validating the quality or validity of the test, or of any evidence that it yields results that are clinically meaningful."

Wouldn't it be great if there were someone in there who would volunteer to take the case on board... and let the patients know? Going private will of course cost more than just the lab fee since the overheads for the practice and consultation have to be calculated in, but the point that is being made here is that although getting tested for HIT will cost money, it does and should not cost a fortune.

It has been pointed out that in the new field of diagnostics of adverse reactions to food it is often quite difficult to get the cost reimbursed in Germany as well as in Austria. Some private insurance schemes have, however, started to incorporate these items into their insurance schemes. This only goes to show how far the rest of us still have to go, if even the Germans and Austrians who are far more advanced in this field are struggling to get these tests on their medical insurance. But it makes sense. Private insurances have a strong interest in getting fast, accurate diagnoses, since then they are likely to have to pay out less for their patients in the long term. They seem to have caught on to the idea.

On the positive side, a most recent development in Austria has been the establishment of the 1st Austrian Out-patient Clinic for Lactose-, Fructose-, Histamine Intolerance and Food Intolerances, which opened its doors to the public at Vienna's Hietzing hospital on 1st September 2009. Their services and tests are covered by the national health insurance funds and they are working closely with the Austrian Ministry of Health in order to inform the general public about food intolerances by distributing information leaflets. The hospital also cooperates closely with the self-help association for Fructose-, Lactose-, and Histamine Intolerance, Food Intolerances and Nutrition, also known as FruLak & Co.

What is currently seen to be a proper diagnosis?

A proper diagnosis is made by a thorough establishment of the medical history and background in combination with testing for diamine oxidase levels and activity. These tests are definitely being offered to a much greater extent by practitioners in Austria, Germany and other European countries. This same degree of awareness obviously seems rather slow in reaching the English language area as of yet, but hopefully it can only be a matter of time.

Clinical tests for histamine intolerance:

- A test for low levels of diamine oxidase in your blood. Depending on the person's threshold and whether the patient has recently eaten food that is low or rich in histamine the test results can vary. Patients have been advised to be on a "normal" diet (whatever they normally eat) before having the blood sample taken.

- A test for high levels of histamine in your blood. Lab tests for histamine need to be done preferably on site since histamine levels can rise due to decarboxylation in the blood. Same principle as with food deterioration.

- A strong reaction to the positive control of an allergy Prick-Test can be an indicator, but is far from a proof of histamine intolerance. A full allergy test is highly advisable to be done by an allergologist since some patients may otherwise be misdiagnosed as histamine intolerant.

- Excluding the possibility of mastocytosis as a cause. Mastocytosis is a condition caused by a presence of too many mast cells in a person's body, and thought to be very rare. Blood tests for tryptase can establish whether the mast cells are very active. If they are continuously active this is an indication for mastocytosis, which expresses itself similarly to allergies and histamine intolerance. Mastocytosis patients have to be on a low-histamine diet for life.

The elimination diet as another option

If you are unable to get the blood test for some reason, then the only other option is first to exclude or establish whether there are any other illnesses, allergies or intolerances and then start the process of a temporary low-histamine elimination diet. This needs to be done under medical supervision. Whatever you do, do not go it alone. Self-diagnosis is not possible and potentially dangerous unless you have a medical degree and are specialised in intolerances and allergies. A provocation test for histamine intolerance is out of the question. You can, as an alternative, take antihistamines (H1 or H2 blockers) for a couple of days, and see if any symptoms disappear. If this is the case you should consult your doctor. Anyone who might tell you otherwise may not have much interest in your well-being but is just spinning you a yarn and is after your money (see "Useless tests – the Commercialisation of Health" below).

You will need to find out, in cooperation with your physician, whether you are basically healthy so that any other factors can be brought into the equation. It is also necessary to do any relevant allergy tests just to include – or exclude - this factor as well. HIT is often seen as a secondary condition in combination with other conditions that affect the digestive system such as those described in chapter two, Morbus Crohn and other digestive disorders. Patients with IBS (Irritable Bowel Syndrome) are also likely to be candidates for HIT. In many of these cases the object of the exercise is to stop the vicious circle. Some lucky people may even see the histamine intolerance disappear at some point, and will then be aware of it should it return for some reason.

How they will determine your medical history, if they don't have it already

The medical expert will need to have access to as much of your medical history as possible, including former diagnostic reports, the medication that you have taken and are taking at that moment, a list of nutritional supplements and vitamins you may be taking, and a list of foods that you are sure you react to badly (food diary) as well as those to which you react well.

How they should be able to establish the likelihood of HIT

In the first stage they will need to ask you about how often you perceive any or several of the following symptoms:

Stomach cramps

Stomach pain

Wind or flatulence

Diarrhoea

Rashes or Eczema

Itching

Flu-like symptoms, runny eyes/nose or sneezing

Headaches

Rheumatic pain

Dizziness

Nausea or vomiting

Extreme tiredness

It is possible that several of the symptoms will apply. This is certainly not unusual. Once the symptoms have been identified you will be asked about the frequency of each one of them.

Possible answers are:

> Occasionally (around once a month or less)
>
> More often (up to around twice a week)
>
> Very often (twice a week or more)

In the next stage it will be necessary to find out if you react badly to certain foods that are known to be the biggest culprits. They are:

> Champaign, red wine, alcoholic drinks
>
> Tomatoes, matured cheese, Pizza, Chocolate
>
> Acidic foods (citrus fruits, vinegar, pickles)
>
> Fruit juices with pineapple, strawberries or banana
>
> Aubergines, spinach
>
> Nuts
>
> Ready meals
>
> Salami or other raw sausage
>
> Shellfish
>
> Glutamate (additive)

Normally you should also have an HIT test done at this point, which, as we have said, can be determined with the help of a blood sample. If you do the test you must absolutely NOT be on a histamine–low diet as otherwise you will get a negative result although you might have the intolerance. The logic behind it is that if you ingest a very low amount of histamine then your diamine oxidase level should, in theory, rise because it is not being used up as quickly. Therefore more DAO will be seen to be around.

The importance of working out a diet

On the basis of these results a professional nutritionist can and should at least be able to work out a dietary plan and give advice on how to keep your diet in balance. If there is no balance in the diet then other health issues may crop up - which is not exactly helpful and will make your life even more complicated than it already is.

I myself have had two tests for my diamine oxidase levels (in Austria). The first result was extremely low. After that I went on a low histamine diet, and returned again for the second test four months later, out of curiosity. The result showed some improvement. Not what I would have liked it to be, of course. Still, the question remained whether the results were really as conclusive as they looked. The fact that I had been on a low histamine diet means that naturally more diamine oxidase was available; it hadn't been used up so fast because I hadn't supplied the histamine. I also had tests done for coeliac disease, lactose and fructose as well as a general allergy test. This established that I also have fructose malabsorption (also known as dietary fructose intolerance).

Most important, though, is that I have been able to track down what the causes of my problems are. I now feel confident that I am in control of the situation and can improve my quality of life.

A WORD OF CAUTION! Some patients may be so desperate that they choose the path of self-diagnosis. This is understandable, since the trust in one's own doctor might take a dive if there are no results and the patient is struggling more and more with general aspects of life, such as work and socialising. But self-diagnosis is a dangerous path to take, especially when there is no background knowledge. The internet may provide some answers and hints, but since every person has an individual medical history the advice offered there is likely to be too general and inaccurate unless given by organisations that are committed to the subject of intolerances. Although some of these organisations are very good and have their own forums, it will not be possible to get a detailed diagnosis through them. What these websites are very good for is to get extra information after the diagnosis, although this is also limited. The interpretation of the test results, all of them, will need to be done by a well-informed professional.

Useless tests – the commercialisation of health

Another big pitfall is companies that may raise your hopes by selling tests that are in no way helpful, except maybe for their bank balance. An article in the UK's renowned independent consumer magazine Which? Magazine illustrates how companies and so-called experts, some even self-proclaimed world experts, are risking the health of patients by promising them test results that will lead to better health through the avoidance of certain foods they claim to have tested for correctly.

IgG Testing

Some labs offer IgG tests for allergies and intolerances. "They use a sample of blood and test it against a range of foods to detect levels of an IgG (immunoglobulin G) antibody. They claim that raised levels of IgG antibodies within your blood indicate food intolerance." Which?'s verdict states that "Although IgG testing is a validated scientific test, our three experts believe that, in line with our findings and other published research, its use in diagnosing food intolerances is difficult to prove scientifically. IgG antibodies are commonly found in healthy people and do not prove intolerance, only that food itself has been eaten. The experts were also concerned that the diets recommended by these tests exclude up to 39 foods – which could lead to nutritional problems."

As it currently stands there are those who say IgG testing works, and those who say it doesn't work at all. What is for sure is that this test does not have any relevance concerning the diagnosis of histamine intolerance and other enzyme-related conditions. People who are not aware of this will be at risk of being put on the wrong diet. It would be a bit more truthful if the companies involved would honestly state what their tests are not for. They tend to otherwise give the impression that they test for everything and more.

Vega Testing

Vega Testing is another of those tests that cannot be applied to testing for intolerances, although it claims to diagnose food intolerances, and sometimes is also advertised as allergy testing – make your mind up, guys - by a method called "electrodermal testing". The person being tested has to hold a metal probe that is connected to a computer, or sometimes to a very strange-looking machine that could be right out of the sixties. Another probe, looking like a kind of pen with a metal point is placed on pressure points next to the nail-bed of one of the fingers. This will create an electric circuit. One by one the tester will put an "essence" of a food substance into the machine and see how high the current reads. If the current is low, they will specify it as a food that needs to be avoided. Researchers from Which? Magazine were told to avoid foods with which they had no problems at all, including wheat (!). Which?'s verdict rightly stated that "Dietician Catherine Collins was particularly concerned that the private practitioner advised Dee (one of the researchers) to exclude all grains from her diet. 'This significantly reduces the intake of fibres, selenium and B-Vitamins, and would make it difficult to get a balanced diet', she said." Neither test for either researcher gave matching results for food intolerances. The authors of the article agree that this method cannot be recommended and Dr Adrian Morris, allergy specialist at the Royal Brompton hospital said: 'Clinical studies have repeatedly shown Vega testing to be ineffective in diagnosing allergies and intolerances'

Hair Analysis

Some companies will try to sell you the story that they can find intolerances through analysing your hair. According to Which? Magazine one of them claims to test intolerances through, "the vibrational energy pattern of your hair which represents the energy state of your body". Another company claims to 'genetically examine the DNA at the hair roots, to investigate food intolerances.' Let's just take the example of histamine intolerance. Could some of these experts, please explain to me how they can test for the amount of or activity of the enzyme diamine oxidase? Don't try unless you have the scientific evidence. It is probably unnecessary to state that the researchers of the article found they were given results that bore no resemblance to their real situation. One of them was told to avoid cow's milk although she has no lactose or cow's milk protein intolerance.

Kinesiology

Last in the row of tests that are absolutely useless, especially for intolerances, is kinesiology. The tests involve lying down and either touching or being close to vials containing food extracts. The practitioner applies pressure on your legs and arms to test resistance. The lower the resistance the more the food is believed to interfere with the body. The authors again found a complete lack of consistency. Results for both researchers show that this technique has no use as a diagnostic tool. They felt that the recommendations given by practitioners were worrying. One of the researchers had been told that she 'would go into shock if she ate peanuts' although she had neither allergies nor intolerances.

Conclusions:

What this article shows is that we need to be very careful with our choice of experts. It can be downright dangerous for people with intolerances and allergies to go down the wrong route because they have been misguided. It prolongs their suffering and may even kill them. Just think of the example of a person who has a peanut allergy but is not told in time because it happened not to show up in the hair, in the muscle tension, or in the energy levels!

From my own experience I can confirm that Kinesiology and the Vega Test were not useful at all. On the contrary, the Vega test proposed a diet containing a lot fruit, and given the fact that I also have fructose malabsorption this would have made me even worse. Good thing I got a proper medical diagnosis on time. Needless to say that neither of the above tests detected either histamine intolerance or fructose malabsorption. I also know a case of a person close to me, who was sent to a kinesiologist by their GP and was given a potion by the kinesiologist after being tested the same way as described above. After taking the potion he started to feel very unwell and decided to go to bed. Most disturbingly, he told me that when he woke up a short while later he was having serious trouble breathing. After this very frightening episode he decided to try other avenues. I rest my case.

5. OTHER INTOLERANCES
DAO AND ITS CLOSEST FRIENDS AND HELPERS

Many of those I have met over the period of writing this book have confirmed something that I did not (want to) believe in the first place. There is the theory out there that HIT never travels alone and that it is normally combined with another intolerance or an allergy. This makes things rather complicated at first, especially when the person affected is still trying to figure out what for heaven's sake is wrong with them. As time has passed I have met a fair number of people with HIT. Not a single one of them that had their symptoms under control was not also suffering from another intolerance or allergy.

Here below are some of the most common intolerances that turn up in combination with HIT. If proof has been established of one of these intolerances by means of a proper diagnosis and some of the uncomfortable symptoms persist, then the GP should also consider testing for HIT. Allergy tests should also be carried out. These tests are carried out for those substances that are commonly found in the different geographical regions.

Lactose Intolerance

The frequency of occurrence of lactose intolerance depends on where you live on the globe. In Africa and Asia between 90 and 100 percent of the population cannot tolerate lactose. In the UK, Ireland, Northern Europe and America it is thought that, on average, about 5 percent of the population have this condition.

Patients with lactose intolerance or lactose malabsorption are either unable to digest this component in milk products, or can only digest it to a certain degree. Lactose is a disaccharide, a form of sugar, composed of glucose and galactose. But lactose first has to be split up into these two components in order to be able to reach the blood circulation via your intestines. This job is done by an enzyme called lactase - let's call it a neighbour of DAO – which is responsible for the breakdown of lactose. The lactose is ingested in the form of all kinds of milk and dairy products.

Someone who has lactose intolerance will either have a very small amount of DAO's neighbour lactase, or have a low activity, or have none of it at all. The consequence of this can be that the lactose will reach parts of their digestive system further down the line from the stomach, where you will find the home of some bacteria. Then there will be a chemical reaction, or more precisely a fermentation process, which will turn it all into large amounts of fatty acids, lactic acid, acetic acid, carbon dioxide, methane and hydrogen. It is not essential to understand what all these chemical components are. It is already enough to understand that they are, in this case, as uncomfortable as they sound, unless anyone thinks that so much acid and gas sounds comfortable.

So how does this discomfort raise its ugly head, you may ask? Well normally by annoying the affected person with diarrhoea, making them feel rather queasy, up to the point of feeling incredibly sick, having painful stomach aches and/or the ever- embarrassing flatulence, also euphemistically described as "wind".

In the past, the only way to identify lactose intolerance was by giving the test person a glass of lactose that has been diluted in water. Should I mention it again, or is it by now obvious how a lactose-intolerant person would feel when overdosing with a large amount of lactose? Anyway, it is still a valuable method, although it has been suggested that it does not always result in a correct diagnosis – but most of the time it should. Another option would be to take a biopsy sample from the gut. Another one of those things that everyone dreads like hell... .

But these days there is a solution to this problem on the horizon, at least for those where it can be proven that they have a genetic predisposition to lactose intolerance. A paper published by the German University in Mainz has argued that the most common reason for lactose intolerance is genetic, and that it can be tested for with a DNA-test called LCT -13910 TT. This theory has been enthusiastically embraced by many, especially those who live in the world of intolerances. Apart from that, this test is easy and much more painless than the ones that have been done in the past as explained above, and it is also suitable for children. This DNA-test can be done with blood samples or cell samples from the lining of the mouth. How wonderful!

So once it has been established then, again, the only way is up. As with every intolerance, the best way to get rid of pain and suffering and embarrassment is to take on the battle and avoid ingesting too much of the culprit - in this case milk products and everything that contains them. Every individual has their own level of tolerance and it is down to them to find out where that is. Some people can tolerate cheese and yoghurt to a certain extent. This is very important to find out, because milk products do provide us with some very important components, most of all calcium. There are several websites and books on the market that provide a lot more specific information regarding what it is all about and how to secure a healthy diet.

Fructose Malabsorption

Dietary fructose malabsorption (also called DFI – dietary fructose intolerance) affects around 1 in 3 people but many of them never realise this as their tolerance level or threshold is higher than their fructose intake.

Fructose is a natural component of fruits and vegetables, although they all have different levels of fructose in them. As a rule of thumb generally, vegetables contain a lot less fructose than fruits and are normally well digested in normal household quantities. Higher levels can also be found in honey, fruit juices, yoghurt with fruit, jams and marmalade, sweets and soft drinks. Fructose, a monosaccharide, is also used as a substitute for normal sugar and can therefore be found in abundance in just about every imaginable low-calorie product or products for diabetics. This is why people with fructose malabsorption have to take extra care when they see the words 'sugar-free' on a package. Sugar–free products often also have another culprit in them – Sorbitol (E 420). Sorbitol can be found in products such as chewing gum, as an additive, and also in some medications. It needs to be avoided because, on top of everything else, it blocks the transport system. The transport system is a protein called GLUT-5 and if the fructose is unable to catch that train for whatever reason, then it will glide further down into the large intestine. There the scenario will be similar to that with lactose intolerance and a process of fermentation will be started.

The symptoms are just as ugly as with the lactose guys. Typically they show themselves as bloating, diarrhoea or constipation and stomach pain. Other symptoms may be a 'fuzzy' head, tiredness and even depression.

Unfortunately there does not seem to be a gene-test around for it. The only way to find out whether you have it is really by doing a fructose test, where you have to drink a glass of fructose diluted in water after a short fasting-period, and you will do a hydrogen breath test measuring your hydrogen and methane levels in ppm (parts per million), which is similar to a breath-test you do when you get stopped by the police. This test should not be done for little children! If there is anything that can be said about the positive effect of having this fructose test, apart from the diagnosis itself, then it is that those who are affected by it will certainly become very aware of what the symptoms are and how they feel. This can be extremely helpful when trying to find out what the personal threshold is, without a higher likelihood of mixing it up with the symptoms of another intolerance.

There is one alternative for those who are unable to do the breath-test, which is to test the stool for it. However, the scientific validity of this method is under discussion. Results of such an examination should therefore be treated with caution.

There is a lot of confusing information out there concerning what you can and cannot eat. Many people think that, when they have fructose malabsorption, they are not allowed to eat any fruit at all. This is not necessarily true. What they need to do is to find out how much they can eat of which fruit. Berries seem to work best with a lot of people. It also works better to have a portion of fruit on the side that can be eaten little by little over the course of the day. It is also quite valuable to know that small amounts of glucose can help with the absorption of fructose, but only to a certain extent, again depending on the threshold of the person. Last but not least it needs to be mentioned that fruits and vegetables also have different amounts of glucose in them, which is why some of them are more digestible than others.

If you have been diagnosed with fructose malabsorption then it is highly advisable to consult a dietician who has a well-founded knowledge of this subject, especially since the components of fruit and vegetables are such an incredibly important and vital source of goodies for our bodies. A properly founded dietary plan will certainly be a great start and help diminish the fear. There are also several websites though, unfortunately, only a few books for the layperson on the market.

Fructose Intolerance

Fructose intolerance, also called "Hereditary Fructose Intolerance (HFI)" is a rare condition where an enzyme (Aldolase B) in the liver which is responsible for the breakup of fructose is defective. This condition is very rare and serious and can be life-threatening. It is not possible for people with HFI to digest fructose and sorbitol, and they will also have to strictly avoid sucrose as well as other substances. HFI can be diagnosed with a molecular genetic test. But this condition should not in any way be confused with fructose malabsorption.

Coeliac disease

Coeliac disease is, in contrast to the above, an autoimmune disease and not an intolerance or an allergy. Around 1 in 100 people have this common problem in the UK and as far as we know around 1 in 200 are affected by it in Central Europe. Sadly it is a condition that, although it is so well known, is still under-diagnosed, but at least the information is out there – and in quantity – which is absolutely fantastic. Just to make sure that there is no misunderstanding here: in common with other intolerances and allergies it is NOT contagious.

People with Coeliac disease share the unfortunate fate of having to avoid anything that contains gluten, a component of the cereals wheat, rye and barley. Some may also have to avoid oats, but that does not apply to all. The problem here is that when any of these components arrive in the digestive system, the immune system starts to attack the lining of the gut. Over a longer period of time this can have some very serious consequences which in turn can have a knock-on effect on other parts of the body.

The range of symptoms are many, but most commonly show themselves in the form of general discomfort, tiredness, diarrhoea and loss of weight, constipation, bloating, loss of appetite, stomach pain, mouth ulcers, nausea, vomiting, aches and pains in muscles, joints and bones, epilepsy, anaemia, headaches, hair loss, skin problems, short stature, osteoporosis, depression, infertility, and recurrent miscarriages.

If you believe that you may have Coeliac disease then you should make your way to your GP and consult with them first. Whatever you do next, you should not stop eating any foods containing gluten before you have had the test, otherwise it will probably show a wrong result, a 'false negative'. The first test will probably be a blood test. If this is negative then, to make doubly sure, you can get a referral to a hospital where a gastroenterologist can take a biopsy of the gut.

At this point I would like to point you towards the website www. coeliac.co.uk. They are a charity for people with Coeliac disease and dermatitis herpetiformis, which is a reaction of the skin to gluten. On their website they have lots of information regarding the specifics of Coeliac disease, how to get it diagnosed, helpful information for those who have been diagnosed, myth busters, information on where to get gluten-free products and where to find them. I stand in awe of what they are doing, just by looking at their website alone.

This is not a curable disease as of yet and those who have been diagnosed will have to stay on a gluten-free diet for the rest of their lives. Fortunately the food industry has caught onto the fact that they can make a healthy profit out of it, which is better than nothing in so far as making the lives of those with Coelic disease "relatively" easy.

Other intolerances with which HIT has been found in combination more frequently than others are casein intolerance, glutamate intolerance and sorbite intolerance.

As can be seen by just looking at the general aspects of the conditions above, it is not surprising that they can be easily confused with each other. This is why it is so vital to find out which ones a patient truly has.

Getting back to my story: When I found out that I had HIT I started to do all the things that were considered to be healthy. I really wanted to get rid of this problem fast. Remember, I had no clue at the beginning, I did not consult a dietician for a while, I just stuck to the list of foods, just the histamine-low diet. Because I was trying to be so healthy I also kept on making myself lovely tasty smoothies. I drank fresh apple juice and tried to integrate more fruit into my self-made new diet plan. But something was wrong. The diet only seemed to work half the time. Sometimes I felt better and sometimes I felt worse. I blamed everything on histamine. Now I know that I felt worse on a day when I had too much fruit for my fructose threshold and that I felt better when I just had vegetables. To be upfront, I had terrible bouts of spontaneous excessively painful farts - the ones where you lie on the floor moaning - with some serious sessions in the bathroom afterwards. Needless to say I was distraught on those occasions. I felt I was losing the battle. I thought I was slowly just going to die if it went on like this. I was scared, and I was very depressed. My mother, who helped me through all of this regardless, was deeply concerned. I could see it in her face, and there was no way I could take the worry from her. We had endless discussions about what could be wrong, what it might have been.

I cannot tell you how lucky I feel to have met several people in Austria who made me aware of the problem of combined intolerances – I know it sounds odd. At the beginning I felt it was a myth, and that "Hey, they are just patients. They know nothing. They make it up as they go along." I was quite disrespectful really, like a cocky little researcher that feels they know it all. But deep inside I was defensive. I did so not want to know whether I had anything else. One intolerance was enough, basta.

Once I was able to pinpoint that in my case it was a combination of the two, HIT and fructose malabsorption, I started the elimination diet with the combination of the two diet plans. That was when I cracked the puzzle. The symptoms finally started to beat the retreat. My intestinal system was finally getting a break and I started to feel a lot more human again. I knew that there was still a long, long road ahead, and that no-one can tell me if either will go away completely, but the main thing was that I knew what it was and that I could actually do something about it.

Looking back at it all now, I sometimes feel very, very stupid. Why did I not listen to what my body was saying?! Maybe I was just listening to the wrong people and trusting a little too much in what others were saying was good for me - and I stopped listening to myself. In hindsight it all makes sense. I can now look back in life and say, "Ah, this is why that happened". Many occasions of feeling ill in the past are a mystery no more, and that gives back a hell of a lot of confidence. I can say that, yes, I may not be able to eat entirely 'normally', but I am not a weird freak or what easily gets passed off these days as a ... fussy eater.

On that note I would like to send out the message to everyone who might frequently use the words 'fussy eater' to describe someone around them. I want to make it very clear that this might have to do with a bad reaction this individual has to certain foods. By telling people, especially children, that they are 'fussy eaters' you are putting them down, being negative and making them feel even worse. Don't do that to them! Without knowing what the exact reason for a person's "fussiness" might be, we have no right to judge them. It is much more helpful to help others find out what the reason for their food fear might be. In principle the concept of 5-a-day and the food pyramid might not be a bad idea, but they just don't suit every single person on the planet. The diversity of cultural and genetic backgrounds alone disallows us from squashing everyone into one food concept straitjacket as if we were machines that all have the same engine and run on the same fuel.

6. WHAT HIT IS NOT

One of the main problems with HIT is that once you start explaining what it actually is, this can very quickly result in misunderstandings. Trying to make it easier for everyone to understand, we tend to simplify - and that is where it can all go wrong. A simple sentence like: "I have Histamine Intolerance" normally meets with the response: "Oh, you have an allergy?" This is not the ignorance of your counterpart, although it may become a little tedious when you feel that you have to explain it over and over - and over - again. To look on the positive side, if you do take the time to explain, you might just spread the vital info so that someone who has not found out yet will at last be empowered and take their first faltering steps on the road to recovery.

Common misconceptions are:

"That's a sort of allergy, isn't it?"

 When you try to explain to people what HIT is, you are bound to use the word 'histamine'. Allergies are strongly connected in our minds with anti-histamines, and for good reason too. This means that HIT is often mistaken for an allergy rather than recognised as an intolerance. Many people who have not been able to identify the cause(s) of their health issues thus run the risk of believing that they might have a food allergy, although they actually have histamine intolerance.

The difference between an allergy and histamine intolerance is that an allergy is an 'over-reaction' of the immune system, whereas histamine intolerance is due to the failure of the enzyme diamine oxidase (DAO) to break histamine down at a sufficient rate. If the real cause of the symptoms is not identified, then the patient is unable to stop a potential downward spiral. In that case, especially if the reaction involves diarrhoea, the condition will get worse and can be the trigger for other conditions, such as other intolerances.

The symptoms of an allergy are very similar and sometimes identical to (mimicking) those created by histamine intolerance. You could actually portray it as a mimicking contest between the two. Allergic reactions can include a runny nose, irritation of the skin, eyes and nose, asthma, abdominal pain, vomiting and diarrhoea - just to name a few. There are three main types of allergies: food allergy; respiratory allergy such as hay fever, rhinitis and allergic asthma; and skin allergies, such as eczema and urticaria. Some people also have severe reactions to medication, latex, pets and stinging insects.

An allergic reaction can be caused by the reaction of the immune system to foreign substances in the body. The immune system's function is to protect the body from bacteria, viruses, cancer cells and other foreign substances. Strictly speaking, allergy is one of five forms of hypersensitivity and is described as a type I (or immediate) hypersensitivity. It is characterised by excessive activation by a type of antibody known as IgE of certain white blood cells called mast cells and basophils, resulting in an extreme inflammatory response.

In the case of an allergic reaction the body will react to information given by the immune system and discharge an excessive amount of histamine and other inflammatory agents. In contrast to histamine intolerance reactions, an allergic reaction is usually within seconds or minutes.

You may, during your quest to track down the cause of your symptoms, have found out that you have some form of allergy in combination with HIT. 30% of allergy patients who are suffering from an inhalation allergy will also report that they have adverse reactions to food. Of these only 10% will have a genuine allergy to certain foods, 10% will suffer from lactose intolerance or fructose malabsorption, 40% will have cross-sensitivities to pollen and 40% of the above allergy sufferers will have histamine intolerance. The advice is thus that those suffering from allergies go on a low-histamine diet during the allergy season.

Those who have an allergy in combination with histamine intolerance will be exposed to something like a double whammy. Following an allergic reaction, or during an allergy season, it is thus even more necessary to stick to a low-histamine diet in order to minimise any symptoms. It is also advisable to support the diet with antihistamines, which are histamine suppressors or inhibitors, during that period. You will need to work out with your GP which anti-histamines are the right ones for you. Try to get some that don't make you sleepy.

"Is this a reason to panic or stop eating?"

The worst thing you can do to yourself is to stop eating! If you have been able to firmly establish, with the help of a doctor, that you do have HIT, yes, of course you will be faced with major and seemingly daunting changes. But to look on the bright side, you will have established the cause of your problem. That is a giant step towards feeling a whole lot better in the future.

There is no reason to panic. Actually, since panic is a severe form of stress and stress releases histamines in the body, it will be an additional task of yours to avoid exactly that. It is not something like a terminal disease; the knowledge acquired by establishing what is "wrong" with you is a great advantage! The only way is up!

"Is this a diet for losing weight?"

The fact that the remedy for HIT is a different, well-balanced diet which is by definition very healthy because of all the fresh ingredients, might give some people the idea that this could be a new form of "fad" weight-loss diet. If you feel that you have problems with your weight then it is best to turn to the vast literature out there that is committed to this specific subject. If you are not feeling ill, then this book is not for you.

7. SPECIALLY FOR THE LADIES – HIT'S FAVOURITE TARGETS

Histamine in women!

A common symptom of histamine intolerance is known in medical terms as "dysmenorrhea". Some women know it all too well as severe period pains.

The majority of people who suffer from HIT are women. Evidence shows it can account for very severe period pains, bad headaches and all kinds of weird and wonderful symptoms from which we females suffer before or during a period. It can also contribute to problems around the onset of the menopause. Since we spend half our reproductive lives either warming up for a period or having one, it's well worth trying anything sensible that would make life more comfortable at that time. Let's first take a look at why HIT sufferers are so seriously affected.

It appears that histamine has a role to play during the week or so leading up to a period – you know, the time those in our immediate vicinity claim we are impossible to live with. This means the less histamine around the better. The diet we have been following for the rest of the month might not be quite strict enough. There's plenty of evidence building up in the chat-rooms that women affected by HIT can reduce the nasty symptoms in that run-up week and during the period itself by cutting back the histamine content of their diet further. The trick is to do this during the week before the period, and not just during the period itself.

Once the lining of the uterus starts breaking down, as it does at the start of every period, the body naturally releases histamines. This can provoke the same symptoms as that notorious glass of red wine or overdosing on tomatoes. Once again HIT sufferers run the risk of an histamine overload. One result of this can be really severe cramps (dysmenorrhoea) that can be so bad you could keel over and wake up in hospital – as I once did. These pains can be so bad that, I am told by those who have experienced both, they make childbirth a walk in the park.

Pregnancy

Talking about pregnancy, it is a well-known medical fact that DAO production, in this case by the placenta, skyrockets from the 3rd to the 9th month to as much as 500 times the normal level. This is why many women identified as having HIT claim that they have never felt better in their lives than when they were pregnant. Nature has a very good reason for the DAO boost. The uterus is very sensitive to histamine and the result of too high a histamine level might be a miscarriage. The bad news is that as soon as the baby is born DAO levels return to your normal level. This means that, as well as all the other stresses and strains of a new baby, delightful as those little tyrants are, you really have to watch your diet too. Serial pregnancies are not really to be recommended as a cure!

Then there's the complex subject of HIT and 'the pill'. If young girls have severe period pains then doctors often suggest going on the pill, or even having an implant that stops the periods altogether. This treatment often works, as it did for me. Like most things in the complex world of HIT, all of this does not necessarily apply to everyone.

Menopause

Although there is no scientific evidence for this yet, there is talk that it is also possible that the decline of oestrogens during menopause may be associated with HIT symptoms. Statistics show that many women around the age of 40 develop HIT symptoms they did not have previously. There appears to be a really complicated link between the hormone oestrogen and HIT. This gives rise to the question of whether there is a link between HRT (hormone replacement therapy) and women with HIT who use it experiencing an improvement in their symptoms. This will be down to the scientists to determine. A way to get through that phase with possibly a lot less trouble and pain will be to make sure that you take special care to eat foods that are very low in histamine.

In short, all those physical processes which make it possible for us to have children affect either histamine levels or DAO production. Knowledge is half the battle. Being aware of what is going on and why it affects us helps us plan our strategy to tackle it. Talking to other women about it, whether personally or through the anonymity of the Net, also helps load up our knowledge bank. Knowing there are so many others out there who want to share their experience and let you benefit from it gives all of us a great big boost. We are not alone!

Until a couple of years ago I thought I was alone in the world with my mysterious symptoms. I shall just relate one example of several similar episodes in connection with severe period pains. I have had severe period pains all of my life, since I was 13, whenever I was not having any hormone treatment. It already began when I started menstruation in my teens. The pain was so crippling that often I would not be able to go to school. Already then, my blood pressure took a regular dive and I was advised to go on the pill. In general, I have fainted – or 'passed out', to describe it more accurately - a lot in my life. But this embarrassing phenomenon has also disappeared since I have been on my individual histamine-low diet.

When I was in my early twenties I was told that I should not be taking the pill for too long. So with some scepticism I decided to give it a try a 'pill pause'. The first month was kind of ok, although still quite uncomfortable. But when I had the second round a month or so later, one morning, after I had been out to party and stayed up late, I woke up feeling what I can only describe as severely ill. My back hurt, my stomach hurt, my legs hurt, I could not think straight, felt cold, shivered, then broke out in a sweat and started to throw up – I shall spare you a description of the ugly rest. I had the idea that maybe a warm bath might help me relax. But it all just got worse. I was on my own at the time and pretty helpless. I only remember crawling out of the bath, but by that time I could not even get to my feet any more. My blood pressure had gone for walkies. This is how I remained, lying on the floor in the hall, until my mother came in the door.

She called the ambulance and I was taken to hospital. There is a faint memory of someone asking me if I had taken drugs. I said I had gone out to party, but no drugs except alcohol and cigarettes. I was in excruciating pain and begged for them to give me anything to stop it. They stuck a needle in my arm and gave me some valium. That shut me up then. At least I stopped yelling. I went to sleep. My mother told me later that one of the nurses told me to stop making such a fuss, because they couldn't find anything wrong with me. My mother yelled at her on my behalf. They did keep me in for 24 hours, by which time I was absolutely fine again.

There were a lot of women in this ward. Some had lost their babies, some had cancer, had their breasts removed. In that short time I learned a lot about what women can suffer. That made me feel incredibly embarrassed about this episode. They found nothing, I had nothing, and I had made a terrible fuss while others were staring death in the face. I never went back to hospital for period pains again afterwards. I just went back onto hormone therapy.

8. HOW DO I FIND OUT WHAT TO EAT OR NOT?

Only when you feel better, will you be able to find out what your body is able to tolerate and what not.

Re-booting the system

The elimination diet will mean that you will need to avoid all foods that are reckoned to be high in histamine and other biogenic amines, and histamine liberators and DAO suppressors - a list of these foods is in the back of this book. You will need to do this for about four weeks. During that time there should be a significant reduction in symptoms. You will also need to take into account that the diamine oxidase (DAO) can be influenced by certain medicines which can inhibit the enzyme, so you should make sure to avoid those too during the elimination diet – but only after consulting with your GP (see section on pharmaceuticals).

After four weeks of avoiding high histamine foods at the latest there should be some kind of significant improvement in your well-being. Once HIT has been identified it is important to stay on the diet for as long as necessary until you feel that your system has stabilised. Only then is it a good idea to move on to the next stage. If your system has not stabilised after this period or you do not at least feel considerable improvement you need to check whether you might have some additional health issues.

Hit and Miss

Next comes the provocation stage, so-called because it means provoking your system to see how much it can tolerate. It is no fun just sticking to the bare minimum of choice of what you can eat and a shame if you miss out on things you might actually be able to tolerate. You just don't know how far you can go. If your DAO levels or activity improve, because, for example, it is no longer suppressed, or your guts got a break from being battered and are able to recover, this may mean that you will gradually become more tolerant to foods with a higher histamine level. Stick to the histamine-low diet that you have been observing and try adding a little of one ingredient at a time. If it makes the symptoms return you will have to try reducing the amount further, or cut it out again for the time being and maybe try re-introducing it again at a later stage. This can be a 'one step forward, two steps back' experience.

Figuring the diet out step-by-step

The provocation phase requires a lot of discipline and patience. When a newly introduced food has not been tolerated very well, you need to wait until the symptoms have disappeared altogether before another new food can be introduced. An upset system will not react kindly to another provocation.

It is also important to keep in mind, especially at the beginning, that eating a combination of foods with higher histamine levels will mean a higher likelihood of symptoms returning. This depends on the individual threshold and process of recovery.

By the time I started to avoid food with high histamine levels I was in such bad shape that I was thankful for any improvement no matter how I did it. It was hard to get my head around the concept and accept that I was no longer able to eat the things I love – at least for the time-being. After all, I quickly realised that before my 'discovery' of HIT I had been systematically munching my way through all the items on the "avoid" list. It was lots of cured, smoked meat, mature cheese, tomatoes, spinach, and bread with added yeast at least twice a day. I still think back nostalgically to how lovely it was, this other life, and even as I dream about it, I seem to have romanticised it all. And talking of bad, let's remind ourselves that under normal circumstances all these food items are not bad for you.

So I went to all the shops and stuck to the list of what to avoid and what is lowest in histamines. At that time I did not think about going to a nutritionist for help. All of this was just a really big nebulous subject to me. My struggle would have been a lot easier if I had spoken to one. Be that as it may, at the time I used my common sense as far as I could. It took me about 6 weeks until my system significantly improved, and that was the point when I started to admit to myself that, actually, this is good for me. I got really determined to make the best of this situation without getting depressed. And it worked!

But my journey has not been without its pitfalls. I remember visiting one of my relatives. They asked me what I could eat. They had bought some tortellini with gorgonzola filling. Sauce was attached with the package. I decided to say it would be fine and that I was much better already. Read the sections on foods to see why that was not a good idea at the time! Maybe it was hope, maybe it was a moment of denial, or my rebellious streak. I reacted really badly to the meal. Within a short time I was going through the worst of my symptoms and ended up in bed. I was distraught. Life would never be the same again, I thought. But I had made a mistake, and at the same time I had done something quite brilliant, while not being aware of it at all. The mistake was that I started to reintroduce something that is one of the highest items on the list – a ready meal – a super-no-no. The positive aspect of this experience was that I now knew exactly what was part played by the intolerance(s) and what I needed to look out for in the future. In the past it was all just a muddle of different and unidentifiable ailments I suffered from. Now I was able to differentiate precisely what was part of intolerance and what was not.

Identifying the whole picture

In my particular case, the symptoms of HIT are actually quite different from those of fructose malabsorption and have a different time-scale too. What they have in common in my individual case is that they both end up affecting the digestive system. Once I had done the fructose H2 breath test and my results were positive, I knew exactly how the symptoms of that specific condition feel, without a doubt. The reaction takes place within one or two hours, the tummy starts to rumble and bubble, I start to feel drained and for sure I will be bolting for the restrooms pretty soon after that. The smell that I leave in my wake is downright embarrassing. It reminds me of the eyebrow-raising smell I encountered when I was a child when we drove past an oil refinery on the way to the airport... well, moving on... . The symptoms of HIT come on much later, normally only the next day, do not affect my upper abdomen, and I also start to sneeze a lot. Remember, this is my personal file of symptoms. Other people will have different symptoms, as has been described earlier.

Being able to separate one from the other, whether it is in connection with other allergies or any other intolerances, can be a great advantage. This helps to unravel the confusion and to gain confidence in reintroducing the right foods and amounts, one by one. Unfortunately it is not always possible to make a clear distinction, but it is worth trying to identify which culprits trigger specific symptoms.

Another instance which keeps on creeping back into my memory is at my mother's place. She continuously left the butter outside the fridge, and the butter would go a little yellow around the edges. She is a wartime child and insisted that this wasn't going to kill anyone and she had been doing this all her life. If you put the butter in the fridge it doesn't spread at all and will just end up in chunks mixed up with bits of bread, and your butty (North country dialect for a sandwich) will just be full of holes, she said. I understood the argument but I was adamant that I didn't like it and I just wouldn't touch it, refused it even... rather have toast without butter. It is one of the many "ticks" that I have developed over the years. Now that we know what is going on, and that histamine is created as part of the aging process of foods, mum has started to put the butter in the fridge for my sake. She'd do anything to help me get better, just like the rest of my family.

Nowadays I generally stick to my list, with the amendments I have been able to make over time. I have actually got used to it, believe it or not, and when I feel really good and adventurous I try to reintroduce another item into my diet. I have had some really nice surprises, as well as the occasional blip. What I have learned is to listen to my body. When it rumbles, I stay away from the new food I tried, and will probably try it again at a later stage. I do tend to do this on weekends only, because if it doesn't work then the next day is all messed up. If it goes wrong then at least I have the weekend to recover and sleep it off.

9. WHAT DO I NEED TO DO AT HOME?

Just to make a little bit of sense of why it is so crucial to keep the kitchen in order and as clean as possible, especially when you start the elimination diet, you need to keep the following in mind:

Histamine is a product of an amino acid called histidine, which in turn is present in most animals and plants. The products that you bring into your kitchen will have certain amounts of histamine, other biogenic amines and histidine in them already.

You will not be able to get rid of any histamine that is already in the foods. Histamine cannot be destroyed by normal kitchen methods such as freezing, cooking, frying, baking or cooking in the microwave. You cannot smell histamine - it is odourless - you can only smell the process of deterioration in a food, like fish. But by the time you can smell that something has 'gone off' histamine levels will have exploded into numbers that have negative effects even on a healthy person.

Histidine could be described as something like the ancestor of histamine. Foods such as cheeses, sausages like salami, beer, wine and vinegar are produced with help of microorganisms. This method is used to bring about the specific taste of a product. During this process the product goes through a certain degree of fermentation, during which histidine is turned into histamine by a process called decarboxylisation. No problem at all for most – bad news for us.

This process also takes place in foods that are in your home. Cooling, chilling and freezing products can slow down this process of decarboxylation considerably, but not completely.

Hygiene

The best way to slow down the development of histamine in your food is to keep the kitchen clean and the food fresh. Foods should be used up as soon as possible and not be left to linger. They should be chilled or frozen. You may need to increase the number of shopping sessions during the week. The fresher the food, the better it is.

The first best thing to do is to take everything off your work surfaces. Give it all a good scrub, and keep it clean. Make it a habit to clean your workspace after you have been cooking and get right into the corners. Dirty, wet cloths, sponges and tea towels are a great playground for bacteria. Make sure to wash them frequently and dry them before the next use. Otherwise you may get into a situation of smearing bacteria all over the place. This will then affect the speed of histamine development in foods.

The fridge is another place where you should take good care. If these places are dirty and your food comes into contact with contaminated areas, the deterioration process will be accelerated, sometimes at a surprising speed.

Out of date – out of your kitchen

Some people tend to leave products that are out of date in their cupboards. Here you can go and have a good cull. Get it all out and have a look at the expiry dates, and get rid of anything that is older than time itself. If you open anything such as, for example, a pot of jam, put it straight in the fridge after you've used it. Again, some people see no harm in putting a jam pot, once opened, back into the room temperature cupboard. It is in your best interest to give up that habit.

Cooking

In the evenings, in the old days, I used to cook, eat and then just slump after a hard day's work. I would put the lid on whatever was left over, leave it on the cool stove, think nothing worse of it and heat it up again the next day if I couldn't be bothered with cooking. So what did I change here? A lot. Nowadays I cook to measure. I will not touch it again if it has been left out of the fridge overnight (someone else, who can cope with it, will eat it for sure).

Freezing

Another alternative to this, of course, is to package the rest in freezer bags, zip them as airtight as possible and put them right into the freezer as soon as they have cooled off. This is a brilliant way of cooking for a week ahead when the day is bound to come where you just can't be asked to do anything after that terribly long day. But try not to leave things in the freezer for too long, as even there the process of food deterioration is not completely halted, but only slowed down severely. Put labels on stuff, with the date, even if it's a bore to do it. If you retrieve something after a long time and you can barely remember cooking it, then maybe it is time to get rid of it. A word of caution here: some people seem to be unable to cope with re-heated food, even from frozen, as their threshold is too low. Foods that are known to have a higher likelihood of a faster growth of histamine levels such as fish and minced meat should not be re-heated at all.

The fridge

The fridge will be your holy kingdom and short-term protector from further histamine development in your food. Make sure when you take something out of the fridge to put it back in again as soon as you can. Products such as milk, minced meat and fish in particular 'go off' at a very fast rate (see also the chapters about milk, meat and fish). Histamine levels can explode into very uncomfortable levels for you. Lids need to be put back on tight. In general, try not to leave anything open in the fridge. I used to leave packs of cheese and sliced meats open. Now I take some kitchen foil and wrap it around the opened package. I also tend to eat up what is in the fridge before I buy anything new. This way I have the guarantee that I cannot forget how old something is and risk placing a ticking histamine bomb in my delicate self.

10.   HOW DO I KEEP THE FAMILY HAPPY?

Cooking for a family of two or more can become a challenge at the best of times. We all go through phases where we are uninspired and reach out to our library of cook books, or try to find new inspiration in the voluminous sections in book stores or by surfing around the web. It is often down to one person, the "chef" in the house, to put something reasonable on the table. Supermarkets nowadays offer a range of ready meals and fast solutions and if we really don't feel like it we can always quickly rush around the corner and get something from the takeaway.

Just one person in the household with food intolerance will, of course, drastically change this very convenient routine. The first trips to the supermarket will become somewhat daunting and depressing unless you go there with list in hand and a specific recipe in mind. As time progresses your confidence and knowledge of favourable products will increase. Even more positively, your best friends and allies will be those fresh ingredients, meaning that your diet will become much healthier and you will stop introducing unhealthy ingredients into both your own body and those of the rest of your family.

Back home you will naturally want your family to share your diet. Some people will be very understanding, but some may not. Why should they stop eating tomatoes just because you are not allowed to have them? Frankly, it wouldn't be fair towards them. There is a way out, though. It might not always be an easy path to stride along but it is necessary. 'Family solidarity' is all very well in theory, but it can evaporate very quickly if someone thinks their favourite takeaway is banned forever. You need to do your own little public relations campaign and arm people with knowledge.

First of all it would be a good idea to gather everyone in a quiet moment and explain to them what it is you have that can make you sick and miserable. Tell them your story. Let them know what you are allowed to eat and drink, and what not and why. It will enable everyone to understand what is going on and why you have been so 'down'. Tell them about the changes you will have to make for a while and highlight the positive aspects. The most positive of all is that after some time you should no longer be the sickly and moody person that you used to be, but regain your vitality. If all goes well then you should hopefully be able to eat more normally again in the future, depending on your progress.

Cooking can be a very sociable experience if you make it that way. It is fun to involve other people, without pressuring them. But they may not always want to join in, and that should be ok too. Give them the freedom of choice. If they want to go out and get a takeaway let them do that, without making them feel they have committed a crime. It will take the pressure off everyone. If they want something different they can cook their own while you are doing yours alongside. You can, for example, make part of the meal for everyone, and they can cook something additional which they like but you are momentarily unable to have. Involve them by letting them taste a little and asking what they think you could improve, if anything. Experimenting together with anyone, whether it is with your family or your friends, can be a lot of fun and also quite inspiring. They will see your new creations and, who knows, since it looks and tastes much better, they might decide they like yours more and eventually lose some of their interest in fast food and ready meals.

Stick your list on the fridge. This may create some interest since you are frequently studying it and your family will read it. Make them part of it all without harassing them, and avoid making them feel guilty about what they eat just because you can't have it. Make them feel that you accept it all with ease, and that you do not feel like an outcast in your own home.

If you make bigger portions - if and when your threshold is high enough after the elimination diet - you can freeze a portion for another meal. This will help save time on those especially stressful days. Freezer bags are a great invention and you can pack it all up pretty well airtight. Make sure to do this as soon as the food has cooled off, not the next day when you have left it outside overnight. However, in order to get the maximum in nutritional value as well as the best taste out of the ingredients, you will fare best by cooking everything from fresh and eating it straight away.

11.   HOW CAN I DEAL WITH THIS AT WORK?

The good news is that, if you had to drop out, you can certainly go back to work once you have been through the worst patch. It is good for you for many reasons. There is nothing worse than sitting at home feeling sorry for yourself. Get back out there into the real world!

The bad news is that you will have to change your habits... quite drastically. Habits are always hard to change, and since this is not just a New Year's resolution, your body and your mind will be eternally grateful for this change. It is a nuisance, but you will not be able to avoid it, so bow to the inevitable, accept it with good grace and get started right away.

The best way to start is to have a big low-histamine breakfast in the morning. This will supply you with plenty of of energy throughout the day. Have a look at some of the recipe ideas, and adapt them to your liking or your medical situation. People tend to snack a lot at work, so how about taking some fruit that agrees with your system and snacking on that instead of the usual crisps and chocolate. I know it's not the same, but it keeps you going. Should there be no shop around the corner, then you can also freeze some yoghurt with or without fruit and take it with you to work. By the time you feel like a snack it should have thawed.

Lunch will be the biggest hurdle in this major reshuffle of your habits. If there is a canteen, then you might get lucky ...occasionally. The dangers of eating in a canteen are the equivalent of a lottery and equally unpredictable. If you do decide to eat there then it will be a good idea to avoid any minced meat, sausages and fish products in particular. They are the ones that deteriorate the fastest. You will not be able to find out for how long these products have been stored, where they have been stored and at what temperature. Without that information you are in the danger zone.

But these are not the only items you should approach with caution. Meals with sauces may have ingredients such as yeast, tomatoes and undesirable additives. Stay well clear of them. With salads it is at least possible to ask for it without dressing, and add olive oil yourself. Milk products may be another obstacle you don't think of right away. Again, the question is for how long has it been stored and where? Milk stood outside in a hot and busy kitchen may not be a problem for others but the histamine level that has developed during that time might be too high for you.

As the German author Thilo Schleip very tellingly points out in his booklet about dealing with and shopping for Histamine Intolerance in that part of the world, any kitchen may be clean and well organised, but if hundreds or even thousands of meals are going out each day, it is bound to affect the condition of the food served. If a plate you like and think you can have looks as though it has been standing around for a while, don't touch it. It is worth waiting for the next batch of plates to come out of the kitchen, even if you feel as if you are starving. Patience is a virtue here and you will hopefully be able to work for the rest of the day without disruption.

For many people the choice is to pop out and pick up a sandwich or a salad. There are an increasing number of fresh and healthy options here, but they are also danger zones for us HITers. How fresh is it? Is it slathered in tomato sauce? Unfortunately, they are a no go area during the elimination diet.

What is the alternative? No, it is not staying at home and wallowing in your misery. How about taking a cold meal with you in the morning? If there is a refrigerator at work then put it straight in there when you arrive, with your name on it, just in case somebody else might get tempted to take it. Some yeast-free crackers can also fill the gaps quite nicely. Fresh fruit is a great option too. When you get home - then reward yourself with a delicious, warm, freshly cooked meal.

12.   WHAT DO I NEED TO KEEP IN MIND WHEN SHOPPING?

Later chapters go into more detail about the do's and don'ts if you are intolerant to histamine. But first I would like to point out some tips and tricks that might help you to dodge your way around the super-market and food shops in general with a minimum of trouble.

Ready Meals

This is why it is a good idea for HITers to stay away from ready meals in general:

Ready meals are almost always made up of many different ingredients – just have a look at the labels, it's mindboggling. Occasionally, as in the 'pot noodle' category, you might wonder if there is any real nutri-tion in them at all!

Let us take a simple spelt noodle dish with a cheese sauce plus ...let's say ham just for the sake of argument. Now, at first sight this looks like something you could easily take home with you. But hold on; let's think about this in detail. Shall we just imagine that we are in a manufacturer's premises where they prepare these ready meals. It is absolutely sparkling clean, which is great. Everyone is wearing their hairnets, their protective gloves and other hygienic clothing. So there is absolutely no hygiene issue here. Let us just imagine that we are in a place where the best and highest possible hygienic and qualitative conditions exist.

In principle spelt noodles should not be an issue for an HITer. After the noodles have been cooked they will pretty quickly be merged with the sauce and packaged. But we have no idea exactly how long they will have to wait until they get united with the lovely sauce. This is poten-tial histamine time-bomb number one.

Then we have the cheese sauce. You will have to ask yourself a lot of questions with this one. First of all; what kind of cheese is it and is it one to be avoided? How long was it outside the cooling system before it was added to the other ingredients for the sauce? How long does the sauce have to wait until it is added to the pasta? Here is potential histamine time-bomb number two.

Moving on to potential histamine-time bomb number three, the ham. You will have to consider what kind of ham it is. Is it just cooked ham?

Or is it ham that has been cured and therefore processed for longer in order to produce a wonderful taste? Remember that cured meats will naturally have a higher histamine count than cooked meats. Again, where was it stored, for how long and at what temperature when it was delivered by the ham supplier? Assuming this factory is adhering to normal hygiene standards, these questions will be of no importance to someone with normal diamine oxidase activity, but they can be of vital importance to you.

Just briefly: checking out the ingredients on the package, if available - as sometimes they like to tell you that you should ask staff if you have any questions about ingredients -, will let you know about any potential histamine-bomb number four, such as undesirable histamine-releasing additives, yeast or soy.

But it does not end here. Potential histamine time-bomb number five could be the actual storage of the finished product before delivery of a whole batch. This is where it moves beyond the manufacturer's control. The products will be moved from the kitchen to the refrigerated lorry and from the lorry to the supermarket, and again from the supermarket storage room to the refrigerated unit or freezer. That can be a long way to go for that kind of product. Any small disruption in delivery and break in the cooling chain can create a 'blip' that can ruin your day.

Number six will be the question of how long it has been lingering in the refrigerated unit or even freezer. And, especially if the product has started to develop a dry blanket on top of the sauce, you will know that the histamines and other biogenic amines will be having a right old multiplication feast, ready to overwhelm your DAO with a stampede.

Additionally, if the hygienic standards in a kitchen are not up to scratch, bacteria will help the histamine to develop and then you will be stuffed. If all is well, then only a few of these factors could contribute to your symptoms rearing their ugly heads in a mild manner. But should you have all these potential histamine time-bombs coming together you will have the big bang. The key here is to diffuse the situation. Avoid ready meals, at least for the meantime. It is a better idea to make a meal at home or find other means for a quick snack.

Canned products

Canned products are mostly unsuitable for HITers. They often have a lot of additives and preservatives that affect us adversely and may also include vinegar, one of the products with the highest histamine levels.

Planning for shopping trips

Arm yourself with a shopping list. The first few times you go shopping you will be certain to feel rather overwhelmed and leave feeling really dispirited. Shopping used to be fun, didn't it? Everyone who is new to a condition affecting their diet is inevitably confronted with this experience. There are thousands of products and checking the labels of only one lane can leave you exhausted and suffering from eye-strain. So the strategy is to plan what you are going to cook at home. Make the list and stick to individual fresh items. Once you have done your basic shopping, and only when you feel up to it, go and have a look at a couple of other items you might be curious about. This is what I call the short and targeted exploration ventures.

It might be an idea to also take the big list of 'suitable' and 'less suitable' foods with you too. Maybe you can print it out in small print and stick it in your purse or pocket, so you always have it with you wherever you go. This can also be useful when going to restaurants, if you want to check whether you need to avoid a certain item, rather than taking a wild guess.

About quality

Whether you go to the supermarket or health food shop, it does not make much difference in how you approach it. The best way to determine the qualitative standards of a shop are by using your powers of observation. Shops that just generally look messy should set your alarm bells ringing right away.

A little bit of research about shops in your area may also bring some positive results while shedding some light on shops with poor standards. You can also check out agencies that monitor food safety or carry out food outlet inspections. They often post results on the web. A busy shop often means fast turnover, which means fresher goods. Look at the freezer, and whether frozen food is stacked above the proper level or if you can see what temperature the food is at. You may not want to buy it, but it is an indication of the attitude of the staff and management. Remember that you cannot smell histamine, so you can't just sniff the level. And if there is an unpleasant 'pong' around you wouldn't want to shop there anyway.

What can be a big advantage is to have access to a food provider who is the first source in the chain, such as a butcher who gets his produce directly from the farm nearby and knows the source of what he sells. Keep in the back of your mind that health food shops may have healthy organic products, but that does not have to mean that these are free of histamine or organic additives that might be unsuitable for you. Talk to your local butcher and/or delicatessen owner about what you need. You'll be amazed how interested and responsive many are.

On especially hot days it may be a good idea to take a cooler box with you, and transport your shopping in there. A cooler box or bag will ensure a relatively unbroken cooling chain, at least from the shop to your home. Some people may choose to use this method of transport all the time, but it is important not to become too extreme, if that is possible. Developing unnecessary hang-ups is a waste of time.

Last but not least, always try to get products that have been made out of the smallest possible number of ingredients. Remember KISS? (Keep It Simple, Stupid.) Let it be your shopping and cooking mantra. Buy local food that is in season. This is the best strategy for getting the freshest products.

Don't let it get you down. It's no use being miserable about it. See it as a quest to get your system back on track as soon as possible. I could, so you can too.

Future quality control in the food industry

What will be especially interesting to people with lower histamine thresholds are the latest research developments. These are particularly concerned with the future implementation of quality control with regard to temperature fluctuations and other data collection during transport of foods. Scientists are currently moving forward in finding the best ways to monitor the transport of food products "from farm to fork". If all goes well, then one day this quality control will include a sensor which can recognise and track the fluctuations of temperature that products have undergone and flag up whether the cooling chain has been broken. One very interesting gadget to look out for is a time and temperature indicator that is actually part of the packaging, visible at the point of purchase. One such indicator changes colour in relation to time and temperature exposure, for example from blue to white, to show whether the food item needs to be eaten immediately or not. This would be relevant for the HIT world. We would at least have some point of reference as to whether a product is still in the condition it was during packaging or whether it has taken a dive in freshness. This, of course, will not tell us anything about the amount of biogenic amines that the product may have had in it from the start. But it would be another little helper in choosing the more suitable products, especially with regard to meats, animal products and other perishables.

The biggest stumbling blocks for the implementation of these gadgets are the interests of food manufacturers. They are sure to point out the expense of having to integrate these sensors into the packaging. But that cost will no doubt be passed on to the consumer one way or another. Some might not welcome the idea of showing how fresh their products are and argue that the information could be misinterpreted. However, once it becomes clear that incorporating such sensors will improve brand image and increase sales, they will be quick to provide them. Last but not least, I also need to make it very clear that I am in no way against the food industry as such. On the contrary, I want to get them on board. The vast majority of them are doing their best to give the customers what they want. They have their problems and we HIT-ers have ours. We are also customers. If there are indeed more than 3% HIT victims in the population, with a peak among women aged around 40 and thus the very people who are shopping for family food, it should make sense to the food industry to cater for us too. They have found ways of doing it for other intolerances. Why not ours?

13.   WHAT CONSEQUENCES ARE THERE FOR MY SOCIAL LIFE?

We human beings are very dependent on one another socially. When we want to relax, we want to go out with our pals and have some fun, leave our troubles behind and forget about the rest of the world... well, maybe that doesn't count for everyone, but it does for most of us.

Friends' reactions to you and HIT will be as varied as the colours of the rainbow. Some people may be concerned and be worried that you could drop off the planet in the next few weeks. The only thing that can help here is to explain to them patiently what it is. You need to emphasise that you are on the mend and that life is on the up and up from now on, but that you will change your habits, at least for a while.

On the other end of the spectrum there are those who feel that you are making a lot of fuss about nothing. They may believe that you have always been a bit of an attention-seeker and that this is just another reason for you to play up a little more and affirm your problems. Some may ask you if it wouldn't be better off getting some psychotherapy – or even just a pet - because it is probably just all in the mind. That is just hurtful, and not helpful at all. If they don't respond to a cool, calm explanation of the facts, then maybe it's time to re-think your friendship. You need all the positive reinforcement you can get, and not to be put down.

There are others who are well-meaning sceptics, who will question you relentlessly about whether you are really sure that you have what you say you have, or whether this is not some kind of confidence trick. They will have read about medications that don't work, false diagnoses and spurious treatments and are worried you might have fallen for one of these. They will not believe you, because they have never heard of this so-called "condition", HIT. Maybe they still think the earth is flat and the centre of the universe. They would probably change their minds if they could walk a mile in your shoes. There will be little point in arguing with them about it – you will only imperil your friendship. Arguing only creates stress, and stress releases histamine. All you can do here is to take a little diplomatic distance, without making them feel that you are insulted, and produce some proof. The results of the temporary elimination diet should do some automatic convincing when it results in your looking better altogether, much more relaxed and at peace with yourself. Remember, they are only trying to help.

Most important are those who listen, who stand by you and are a pillar of support during a substantial period of change. They may not understand it all, but they give you their trust. They are the best and you will recognise them immediately. One day there will be the chance to do something in return for what they have given you: an open mind and a lot of understanding.

Once again I would like to point to my own experiences. Generally speaking, I can confirm that all my friends only want the best for me. But everybody reacts differently according to their personality and their own experiences. I have struggled with criticism and being questioned, especially when I didn't feel like talking about it for the ten-thousandth time and just wanted to be left in peace. When I get really fed up, I just tell people to go and have a look on the internet at the research which has been carried out, peer reviewed and published by some highly respected scientists. I have had an immense amount of support, also from friends from whom I did not expect it. This was incredibly important and has strengthened many relationships which I hope will last a life-time. These people are invaluable to me and I will never be able to return what they have given to me – and I let them know this in various kinds of ways. This does not have to be expressed verbally, but by returning the favour and standing by them when they are going through their own difficulties, whatever those may be.

Going out

There are different situations that need to be confronted. All of them can be handled. Things might become a bit more complicated. But the worst you can do to yourself is to stay at home and roll up in a sad little ball although you really feel like going out with the mob and having a good time. If you feel physically unwell it is, of course, another matter. There are some pitfalls I would like to point out. Learn from my mistakes! I was pretty new to the situation when I first knew I had HIT. I had to learn that things are not always that easy when you go to a bar or pub.

The most challenging of all was when people, who had no idea that I had had to change my ways, asked if I wanted a glass of wine. I had come to the bar with the conviction that I would not drink anything but a suitable soft drink, and out of the blue, when I was asked the magic question, this little monster would creep up inside me, saying, "Come on...you can have one. Just one. Can't be that bad...come on." And after a long struggle I would say..., "Yeah, why not. Just the one." It was a big mistake at the time. I had to leave pretty soon afterwards, feeling that my symptoms were building up. I went home, felt depressed and spent the rest of the evening in front of TV - and the next day mostly in the smallest room of the house. Obviously the conclusion here is that this is not the way to go.

Our social habits are so much part and parcel of our culture that it seems almost unacceptable not to go with the flow. We (in my Western society) feel that we are not part of the crowd, may think that we are not being sociable enough, or even boring, if we are not drinking alcohol. I am not saying that people in general should not drink alcohol in moderation. It should be down to the individual whether they want an alcoholic drink at any point in time, and in the case of HITers this should be done with great care in order not risk a backlash. It is a shame when you have put a lot of time and effort into getting better and it is temporarily ruined by something as banal as social pressure. Been there, done that.

These days, after a long and strict diet mixed with provocation periods, I am absolutely able to enjoy the occasional alcoholic drink.

People around you get used to your 'abstinence' pretty quickly and stop asking at some point. The shortest answer I have come up with personally is "I cannot tolerate alcohol at the moment. It makes me feel ill, but thank you so much for offering". That should stop everyone in their tracks and hopefully cut out the discussion.

Going to the Restaurant

Going out to eat is a whole different deal. It is initially very, very difficult because of the many factors that have to be considered. A suggestion would be to cut out eating at restaurants for the period of the elimination diet. Afterwards, give it a try. As always, it all depends on your personal threshold. Salads are less of a problem because you can ask for them to be served without tomatoes and vinegar. Soups may have been made fresh but are often made with a stock base which can contain MSG (monosodium glutamate), yeast or soy. With regard to sauces, it is a good idea to ask for these to be served separately, giving you the choice of adding no sauce at all or just to have a taste. You don't know how long different ingredients, such as milk products, meats and especially fish, have been out of the refrigerator before they hit the pan. Deserts often include the very fruits that are on the list.

Restaurant quality

You will also need to be aware of the quality of the restaurant. Here is what the UK's Food Standards Agency says about danger signs:

Dirty public spaces (if the areas you can see aren't managed well, imagine the state of the areas you can't see)

Dirty tables, crockery, cutlery and glassware

Staff with dirty hands or fingernails, dirty aprons or long hair that isn't tied back

Overflowing garbage bins or bags of rubbish outside the premises (these could attract pests and flies)

Dirty toilets and washbasin areas

Raw foods displayed next to cooked foods or the same serving spoons or tongs used for both

Food on display that has passed its 'use by' date

Hair or insects in food

If you spot any of these, there is a good chance that standards of hygiene are not what they should be and you might want to think about taking your business elsewhere.

But all is not lost. If you want to go out in the evening you can, for example, try to stay on a low histamine diet for as long as you believe is necessary, take an anti-histamine before you set off for the restaurant and then choose a meal that looks least likely to do you any harm. You may not be able to do this every day, but it is a way to occasionally step out of the routine. You need to remember that taking an anti-histamine only suppresses the symptoms of histamine, but the histamine itself will not dissolve miraculously because of this. When histamine passes through the barrier in your intestines, for whatever reason, then the job of breaking it down will have to be taken over by other mechanisms in the rest of your body. These mechanisms, such as the metabolisation of histamine by N-Methyltransferase, already mentioned previously, will however, be far from as efficient, and will therefore take much longer to deal with the overflow of biogenic amines. Therefore you need to take special care here.

The positives and negatives of the DAO enzyme supplement

Another option would be to take the enzyme in the form of a tablet. "Oh," you might say," so there's a tablet! Why didn't she tell us this before then? We can just pop the pills to make up the deficit, much like a diabetic does, and get on with our lives." The simple reason why I am not recommending that you do this is because, as yet, there is not the scientific evidence to show what the long-term effects might be. So, as far as I am concerned, once in a while is fine but as a permanent solution – not yet!

The first question is whether you are able to obtain them, because they are not readily available everywhere. Apart from this, they should be taken in consultation with your medic and really be taken with caution because they have not been on the market for very long and no-one can really be sure whether they might in any way affect a possible (partial) recovery from HIT. The question is whether a long-term increased intake of these enzymes could possibly trick the body into thinking that it may not need to produce them itself any longer. In that case, this would be potentially quite dangerous and also lead to a dependency on the tablets. The manufacturers do give notice that their "product is not intended to diagnose, treat, cure or prevent any disease".

The supplement has been used as part of what is called an enzyme therapy. It has been mentioned that in some cases the tablets have been applied alongside diets and that there has been an improvement of the condition afterwards. However, there is as yet no properly founded independent scientific evidence to back this up, therefore there is as yet no proof.

I have these tablets, have taken them for a short while after the diagnosis, but only when I felt that it was really, really, really necessary - usually when I went out on location to film. Personally I prefer not to take these enzymes except in emergencies, because I think they mask the underlying cause, when what you should be doing is establishing your own levels and, by means of diet, giving your body a chance to recover naturally. I would really, really welcome some proper scientific research into the effect of these pills in the long-term. The tablets are very expensive, and someone on a lower income couldn't afford them for long-term use. Vegetarians would probably automatically opt out of this solution because the tablet ingredients have been extracted from pigs' kidneys.

There have been some complaints. There have been some reports from sufferers I have spoken to who say that, for some reason, the tablets only work sporadically for them. This may have something to do with another health issue involved, or that the enzyme ingredient may be exhausted when a lot of histamine-rich food and drink is ingested. It may also have something to do with the tablet not having been taken at the right time. The manufacturer says that it should be taken 15 minutes before the meal. Experience suggests some fine-tuning is necessary in individual cases. Any histamine-rich food that has been ingested before the capsule starts to work will not be metabolised by the DAO from the tablet. The scientists will have to sort this out in future. All in all the tablets are not the optimum solution from the consumer point of view. The manufacturers claim that "Europeans have used this formula for years with rave reviews." Have they conveniently forgotten about those who were not so happy? The supplement seems to have a positive effect for patients with a slight degree of histamine intolerance, but not for those who have severe histamine intolerance, so hold your horses. Whatever else, it is neither a 'magic bullet' nor a 'get out of jail free' option.

Reintroducing little by little according to threshold

Don't forget that your threshold may rise as time goes by and that you can, if you feel up to it, carefully test out how far you can go. The trick is once again to keep it simple. Do not have too many ingredients you need to avoid at the same time, and don't have too much of any single one... like a plate of tomatoes... or red wine with a selection of cheeses. If you stick to that you may be able to include more and more of your favourite food components in your diet again, as I did over time. But it is unfortunately not a guarantee that everybody can do this.

By now I have reached a threshold where a visit to a restaurant is much less of a problem. I can't claim that it has always worked out positively, but I have been able to go on several trips, including some for work, where I have been eating in restaurants regularly and have only experienced the occasional mild symptom which could be sorted out the following day. The main difficulty is that it is not possible to define the overall histamine levels. But the knowledge of how histamine develops, where and how fast, as well as having the food list, is a huge help in assisting you in making some educated guesses at what is best to choose from the menu. It is hard to describe, but I have developed my own instinct for what to choose and what not, what is safer and what is more risky. Of course it doesn't give 100 percent protection, but it is good to have.

The journey is the reward!

14.   MEAT - THE GOOD...THE BAD AND THE UGLY

Meat is a great source of protein, minerals (iron, selenium and zinc) and B vitamins. It is the higher levels of protein in the meat that contribute to the development of histamine. The packaging, as well as the storage and the path from the slaughterhouse to the till, are important factors that need to be taken into account here.

Your quest will be to search for the freshest articles that you can find. If you do not happen to have a butcher just round the corner, then your search for hidden treasure will be limited to the local supermarket. It is always a challenge to combine your working day with shopping and cooking, but for the sake of your well-being the detective work will pay off.

Meat, like fish, has very low histamine levels when it is fresh. That is the good news. But in a supermarket you are unlikely to be able to find out exactly when the animal was slaughtered, nor how long the meat travelled before it got to you. If you are restricted to supermarkets, then look first in the freezer. It is your best bet of locating the least histamine-rich items because here the opportunity for histamine to develop has been reduced to the minimum. If you find something tasty in the freezer, then dig deep to see which package has the longest expiry date. If the packaging is punctured or damaged, leave it alone. In general, though, remember that unfrozen, really fresh meats have low histamine levels.

The perfect situation is to have a butcher's shop near you. It is even better if this butcher has his own local farm providing most of the meat. He should be able to tell you exactly when it was slaughtered and how long it has been with him. Talk to the man (or woman, of course!) in charge, in a quiet moment when they are not stressed. Butchers normally like to be asked questions. Many of them have been in the industry for a very long time, perhaps even for generations, and they are proud of what they do. They have a wealth of knowledge and most of them will be happy to share it with you. Briefly explain your problem to them and maybe even throw in that, as in the case of an allergy, you suffer if you don't stick to the rules. Appeal for their help.

Many reputable butchers in the UK are members of the National Federation of Meat & Food Traders. Those retailers are subject to quality inspection at any time. If the butcher fails to meet the required standards they will simply not be re-invited as a member the next year. Proof of membership can be found in the form of a sticker at the butcher's shop or on the NFMFT website. You can also get information directly from the NFMFT headquarters on legislation as well as technical data on seasonings that are added to butcher's products such as, for example, sausages that are freshly made on site.

Here are some guidelines on buying meat:

Chicken and Turkey

Chicken needs to be purchased within 2 days of slaughter. It will be one of the freshest products you can get. Thumbs up for this one, but also beware since it can deteriorate at horrendous speed under the wrong conditions.

When chicken is packaged, check the dates as always. Check if the chicken is from a local source, or whether it comes from further afield. There is a difference between the labelling "Country of Origin" and "Country of Manufacture". The country of origin may be in one country, let's say Belgium, and the country of manufacture, where it has been handled and packaged, could be in the UK. This would mean that the meat has travelled a long distance to get to you, with some processing stations in between. If you see that a label says "manufactured in the EEC" it is very likely that the meat has travelled quite a distance from another country. The same principle can apply for other meats, especially for pork.

Pork

Pork, too, is normally delivered to the counter pretty rapidly since it does not improve with age. Smoked bacon and cured bacon have of course been processed for a period of time, which means it is definitely not advisable to have this on your plate, at least for now.

Sausages

There are sausages and sausages. The good ones and the bad ones. The good ones are those you can get from the butcher. They will be the nearest to the natural product you can obtain. Ask about additives and see if there are any you may not be able to tolerate. If they are home-made and if he has fresh supplies made on the day then they are really fresh, flavoured with lovely herbs and spices. It is advisable, though, to wait until you get to your provocation phase to try out sausages because they are made of minced meat (see below). Packaged sausages and canned sausages in particular are not advisable. Apart from the fact that some of them include ingredients such as MRM (mechanically recovered meat) and yeast, you will never be able to know how long it took the final product to get into the tin and under what conditions. These sausages might be suitable for anyone without HIT, but it is better for you to stay away from them unless your condition improves greatly.

Minced meat

Minced meat should be absolutely fine for your diet as long as it is as fresh as you can get it and thrown straight into the pan. The issue here is that because mince has a larger surface area, so much more of the meat is being exposed to oxygen. In the right (wrong) conditions the production of histamine will be vastly accelerated. Pork should be given preference to beef only by those with the most severe cases of HIT. A good butcher will follow your request to grind some fresh minced meat from meat that comes straight out of the cooler, rather than that which has been on the counter for a while. Do not re-heat cooked minced meat.

Beef

Beef normally gets hung for at least one to two weeks in order to get the best out of it. Those who are extra, extra sensitive need to take this into account. The colour of the meat does not indicate the chemical distribution. If this meat is kept at the correct temperature in the correct environment then there is minimal microbial action.

Cured meat and raw cured sausage, liver products

Due to the lengthy maturation process and the development of other biogenic amines it is advisable to avoid these products. Examples of these are Salami, cured ham and beef or Parma ham. Sad, but true. Try cooked ham or cooked turkey instead of the smoked or cured variety. The taste of raw cured sausage is created through fermentation with bacteria such as lactobacillus. Because of the nature of its processing it is something to be especially avoided by people who frequently suffer from digestive problems. It is also highly advisable to avoid liver or liver pâté, because they contain higher concentrations of histamine. If any of these have been a part of your 'normal' diet then check with your dietician to make sure your diet remains balanced.

Hitting the road with your shopping

When you have purchased your item of choice then it is best to take it home and put it straight into the refrigerator before you do anything else. The worst you can do to yourself is to leave it to bake in the car for an hour or two because you decide you want to go for a chat with a friend in the tempting sunshine. It is also a good idea to put meat in a separate compartment or shelf at the bottom of your refrigerator, just in case the package is leaking and drips onto your other products. If you see that there has been some leakage then give the compartment a good clean. Make sure the refrigerator stays clean anyway. This keeps the bacteria at bay and lessens the histamine production even further.

Storage

Once opened, make sure to wrap your meat products up again in foil or film as airtight as possible to avoid contact with the outside atmosphere. Wipe any places that might have come into contact with juices, as this is a source for bacteria to grow and this will again accelerate the histamine development in any other food it could have contaminated.

Freezing is great. If you are not using it the same day, freeze right away as soon as you get it out of the shopping bag. Frozen products can be a good solution for some of us since the meat should have been frozen in a controlled environment and the development of histamine has then been slowed down by the reduced temperature.

The recommended temperature for household refrigerators is between 1°C and 3°C. For household freezers an average temperature of -18°C is recommended. What many of us forget is that if you open the refrigerator, even for a very short time, there will be a sudden rise in temperature. Also, when you overload the refrigerator or freezer with a large volume of produce after your shopping trip, the temperature will rise significantly. The rest of the contents of the refrigerator will warm up slightly and it will take a little time for the refrigerator to cope with it. To keep track of the temperature in your cooling devices you can buy a suitable thermometer with a digital display at the pharmacy or DIY store.

15. FISH - THE GOOD... AND THE UGLY

Fish in general contains a very useful spectrum of different goodies the human system needs, such as proteins and minerals. Oily fish in particular provides us with a higher degree of Omega 3 fatty acids together with Vitamins A and D than does white fish. Having a little fish every now and again, preferably twice a week, will definitely do you no harm. The drawback here is that fish generally contains high levels of histidine, (see below). If fish is not stored properly or in unhygienic conditions where it comes into contact with bacteria, it will result in just the right environment for histamine levels to explode, especially in warmer climates. And this can escalate to extraordinary levels within a very short period of time.

There are several ways of avoiding this problem.

Fresh fish that has come right out of the water contains hardly any histamine. So, for us, this means that there is no reason at all to avoid it in the principle. If you want to have the security of histamine-low fish, how about a trip to the seaside at the weekend? One of life's great experiences is to walk along the beach early in the morning – keeps you fit and is relaxing at the same time. Then go to the fishmonger and see what he has caught on the day and take it straight home in a freezer bag with ice in time to start cooking lunch. Afterwards, a relaxing nap in the afternoon. Just a thought.

Let's go back to the serious business of daily life. The reality is that a lot of us only occasionally have the time to travel many miles to another place far away and do this kind of thing. A fish fan will need to be aware of the following: always keep in the back of your mind that the amount of histamine in fish and shellfish depends on how it is kept cool and stored during the interval between the fish being caught and being eaten.

Packaged and frozen fish that has been treated according to the rules and regulations should be absolutely fine. I bought some frozen fish from the shop-freezer at the start of my journey home. Since I only wanted to cook it in the evening I took it straight home, let it thaw a bit in the refrigerator, and cooked it shortly after. I took extra, extra care to keep the kitchen clean, just to make sure nothing went wrong - and it was wonderful. I noted down the details of the product and where I bought it and had thus added another food to my ever-growing list of things I have been able to tolerate. Of course, conditions during fishing, the time that lapses between catching and gutting the fish and from then until packaging, as well as standards of hygiene, can vary for the same product. Keeping track of good experiences is one way to try and get a consistent supply of a quality product. A company working to high standards is likely to keep it that way, although there is of course no guarantee.

Fish from cooler climates tends to develop less histamine than fish from warmer regions, such as tuna and sardines, but in general all freshly caught fish initially contain extremely low levels of histamine.

Scromboid poisoning

Scromboid poisoning is a very serious condition for anyone and typically occurs after the ingestion of fish that is no longer fresh or has even been contaminated by bacteria, especially tuna, bonito and mackerel, because of the excess levels of histamine the fish contains. As mentioned previously, histamine and other amines are formed in food by the action of decarboxylases, produced by the bacteria that act on histidine or other amino acids.

At a seminar on histamine at the Maui Community College at the University of Hawaii Dr Steven Farmer an Internal Medicine Physician said that "Scromboid food poisoning is the principal chemical agent type of food-borne disease found in the United States: the second most common is ciguatera poisoning." This is just an observation that applies to the USA, but it could easily be reflected in the rest of the world since hygiene, as well as storage and length of transport times of products, is an issue affecting not only the USA. This raises the question of how many people with HIT are included in the cases of food poisoning that are known to us. Surely those who suffer from this condition are incredibly vulnerable.

Scromboid poisoning has been associated with a number of other foods, such as Swiss cheese. However, it is more frequently associated with fish, especially if the fish has not been gutted on board and frozen rapidly after being caught.

Shellfish

Shellfish should be avoided altogether for a while as it is highly likely to contain a higher level of toxins as well as being vulnerable to the rapid development of higher amounts of histamine & Co. as soon as it is taken out of the sea. Apart from scromboid fish poisoning there is also the possibility of shellfish poisoning, which is caused by toxins manufactured by algae that accumulate in the shellfish. This may cause intestinal illness, which a sufferer from HIT cannot afford, since this will affect the function of diamine oxidase in the gut.

Preserved fish products, canned fish, smoked and marinated fish.

Here we move straight into another danger zone. During the elimination diet in particular it is very, very advisable to stay away from these products. The fact that they have been through a complex and often lengthy manufacturing process, giving rise to all kinds of histamine-creating opportunities, and that they could contain additives such as, for example, vinegar or yeast, makes them a highly likely candidate for raised histamine levels. At a later stage you could consider tentatively trying those products that do not contain any of the ingredients (eg. additives and yeast extract) that are to be avoided in general.

Personally, I have stuck to the fresh fish - because I am not willing to take the risk and undo all my good work. I am hoping though that one day there will be a possibility of a home test for histamine in food. You will be wondering how I got that idea, I am sure, but during my research I uncovered some very interesting information.

Will we be able to measure histamine levels at home in future?

A research team, led by the University of South Carolina's Dr. John Lavigne, created an instrument resembling a disposable "dipstick" that would quickly determine if food will make you sick. It could be generally available within a few years.

In an interview, Dr. Lavigne, explains: "The basic concepts behind the dipstick tests that we have developed is based on a polymer that we have made in our lab that pretty much turns colours in the presence of different biogenic amines. These biogenic amines are formed by the bacterial spoilage of different foods. In our lab so far we focus primarily on fish, but the same approach can be used for different meats, fruits, vegetables, beer, wine, nuts. It covers pretty much any food that has protein in it. And what we are measuring is the decomposition products of that protein as the bacteria acts on the foods. Basically in one format the polymer changes from purple, which is good, to red as it starts to get bad to a more yellowish colour as the food spoils further. We've really focused on the consumer, the individual consumer where it is a type of a device that can be used at home, or in a restaurant perhaps even. My interest stems a lot from food poisoning. I had eaten some leftovers, they smelled fine, they looked fine, but still there was the bacteria present, these compounds were being formed that I could not yet detect."

"One of the approaches that we have had is to develop a kind of - either a card or something about the size of a credit card, or in the order of a pen or a pencil, where the devices can extract a small amount of liquid from a solid sample like a fish pâté that can then develop the test, and you could simply read it off the card as being yes or no, good or bad. Analysis there is similar to a home pregnancy test, or similar also to the analysis done by diabetics when they test their blood glucose."

Some useful tips from the Food Standards Agency

Buying fish:

Buy seafood from reputable sources. Be wary of people selling seafood out of the boot of their car.

Choose fresh fish or shellfish that is refrigerated or on ice.

When you're shopping, pick up fish and shellfish last and take it straight home.

Don't buy cooked fish or shellfish (such as shrimp or crab) that is in the same display case as raw fish and shellfish because these should always be kept separate.

Don't buy frozen fish or shellfish if the packaging is damaged in any way.

Don't buy frozen fish products that are above the frost line in the shop's freezer.

Don't buy frozen seafood if you see ice crystals or signs of frost through the packaging. This could be a sign that the fish has been stored too long or that it has been thawed and refrozen

Storing and preparing fish and shellfish:

Put fish and shellfish in the refrigerator or freezer as soon as you get home.

Make sure that all fish and shellfish are covered or wrapped.

Don't store fish or shellfish in water.

Discard shellfish if their shells crack or break. Live shellfish will 'clam up' if their shell is tapped.

Wash your hands before handling fish or shellfish.

Thaw fish or shellfish in the refrigerator, preferably overnight, or if you need to thaw it more quickly, you could use a microwave. Use the 'defrost' setting on the microwave and stop it when the fish is icy but flexible.

Use separate cutting boards, knives, plates, etc. for preparing raw fish or shellfish.

Don't allow raw fish or shellfish to come into contact with cooked foods.

Cooking fish:

Cook fish so that the fat drips away.

Bake, poach or grill fish, and don't use the fish drippings.

Marinate seafood in the refrigerator and throw the marinade away after removing the raw fish or shellfish.

Further information on the subject of fish can be found at:

Food Standards Agency:	www.eatwell.gov.uk
Marine Conservation Society:	www.mcsuk.org
Marine Stewardship Council:	www.msc.org

16.   MILK AND DAIRY PRODUCTS – ESSENTIALS

For milk and dairy products, in common with all other animal products, much depends on the manufacturing process, the manufacturer's standards of hygiene and the degree of fermentation, or in other words the ripening stage. With these products, too, you will need to be disciplined about your storage habits. It is best not to leave milk and dairy products outside the refrigerator for too long. Every time the products get taken out of the refrigerator into the warmth for any length of time the histamine count will rise.

Milk products are a great source of Vitamins A and B12 and also supply you with calcium which is important for your bones. It will be important to discuss with the dietician how much and which products you should incorporate into your diet as a minimum. As with other food groups, your dietician would help you find alternative sources to make sure that your elimination diet will not have any negative long-term consequences. It will not be enough just to pop in some calcium pills bought from the supermarket. Do, please, talk to the professionals about it.

Your best friends will be - if you happen not to have lactose intolerance as well - fresh pasteurised milk and the freshest possible ricotta, cottage cheese, quark, butter, cream and sour cream, yoghurts without the addition of any items or flavours on the "avoid" list, and any other similar fresh young, immature cheese products. Most of these products should be safe, with fresh milk and ricotta especially suitable for the hypersensitive. Yoghurts have been subject to discussion but have been viewed positively by many. The amount of histamine in yoghurts depends on, for example, how the individual product has been inoculated with histamine-producing bacteria and length of production or fermentation. It is up to you to find out which yoghurt is suitable, but certainly worth investigating. Best would be to start by testing with small amounts. Nowadays there are an increasing number of lactose-free products available on the market that have resulted in positive reports by patients, with one company even claiming its product is histamine-free. A more substantial conclusion will certainly be possible sometime in the near future.

When you are finished with the elimination diet it is safest to start by re-introducing young, immature cheeses such as mild Gouda. Other cheeses you can try out include Mascarpone, Mozzarella, Bonbel,

Feta, blue cheese, and mild cheddar. You will have to test, one by one, whether you can tolerate some of these. It may be a good idea to talk to those at your nearest delicatessen, as long as you can assure yourself that they have a good knowledge of their cheese products. Once again, if you have found a certain cheese product that you are able to tolerate well, note it on your list, together with the manufacturer. Different manufacturers will have different ways of handling their products, but it is more likely that one manufacturer will consistently maintain the same process for the same product in order to retain quality standards.

Less mature cheeses also tend to have less histamine

Older, more mature cheeses will have a high, sometimes extremely high, histamine count. Cheeses that have been ripened for a long time will probably not be an enjoyable experience for an HITer, depending, as always, on the individual threshold and how far someone has been able to recover through the change of diet. This means that eating the likes of mature Cheddar, Brie, Edam, Parmesan or Raclette cheese will most likely trigger some very uncomfortable reactions for those with a low threshold.

Raw milk products should be avoided. The risk of a potentially harmful gastro-intestinal disease is very high here, because raw milk and its products are highly susceptible to bacterial contamination which in turn can make you very ill. Because of this it is also possible for the development of histamine to accelerate to extraordinary levels. The sale of raw milk and its products is heavily regulated in many countries. In Scotland the sale has even been legally prohibited.

There is plenty of scope for imaginative recipes using cottage cheese, ricotta and yoghurts. At first, when I had a close look at the list of what I had to avoid, I was in a state best described as a mixture of mild shock and super-frustration. That's the only way I can describe it. Being half Dutch, half English my background consists of two cheese-loving nations. Until I had to change my ways I was enjoying cheese a lot, in all variations and at all stages of ripening. The variety of cheeses I ate was enormous in comparison to now. I had no other choice but to look around for alternatives and started to experiment with what was permitted. It is possible to make some wonderful salad dressings using yoghurt, which gets you around the vinegar problem, as well as using yoghurt in sauces that give you something tasty to dip into with your main meal. My favourite is Tzatziki with loads of garlic, or some quark with the fresh herbs that grow on the window-sill or in pots outside in the garden - unless the slugs get to them first.

I was able to re-introduce Mozzarella in several stages, as well as Feta (in small doses, though, not a whole pack at once), and young Gouda. After a year I was able to use a bit of grated Parmesan, just for the taste.

One of the most important things to remember about cheese is that, although stored in a refrigerator, it will slowly but surely age. The more mature cheese is, the more unsuitable it becomes for someone with HIT. For now I have stopped buying several pieces of cheese at a time for myself. I just buy a small portion, and when it's used up I get a new, fresh one of a different sort.

17.   FRUIT & VEGETABLES - THE LITTLE LABYRINTH

Nearly all vegetables and fruits are low in histamine although this depends, as always, on the ripening stage of the individual item. There are, however, some exceptions. What you will have to watch out for here are three different symptom triggers. We will have to split these into different categories. Trying to read your way through the scientific papers and their theories can seem a little like a journey through a labyrinth. So here, hopefully, is the simplified version.

The categories are:

Fruit and vegetables that tend to contain a higher level of histamine

Fruit and vegetables that contain a high level of other biogenic amines, raising the likelihood of your DAO enzyme being overwhelmed one way or another

Fruit and vegetables that liberate histamine stored in your body

Fruit and vegetables that tend to contain a higher level of histamine

Those vegetables with the most significantly high histamine levels are tomatoes, spinach, aubergines, avocados and soy. A more comprehensive list, according to the latest knowledge, is to be found in the back of this book. Once you have finished your elimination diet and feel comfortable with it, you can then try to reintroduce these foods one by one. It is down to each individual to find out to what extent they can tolerate any of these on top of the level of histamine and other biogenic amines they have acquired through all the other sources.

Some preliminary research studies have indicated that histamine may be produced during ripening in tomatoes. It may be that some, if not all, fruits that go through a similar process also produce histamine as they ripen. It remains for future research to explain this phenomenon.

A quick detour to the subject of legumes and nuts

Some research into peanuts, a member of the legumes family, has indicated that "histamine concentration is 0.08-0.56nmol per 100g of raw peanuts compared to 35-150nmol for 100g of roasted peanuts".

Fermentation processes are likely to generate a large quantity of histamine. This could explain the differences in the intensity of the disorders occurring after ingestion of the same quantity of peanuts. Histamine appears to increase in peanuts the longer the storage time. You will need to test out whether you can eat peanuts at all. On the subject of nuts, what you will need to avoid, at least for the period of the elimination diet, are cashew nuts and walnuts. They have a generally higher level of biogenic amines. Beware of any nuts that might have been stored for too long or which may have gone rancid. It will be best to use up any nut products as quickly as possible rather than leaving them hanging around somewhere for a year or two... as we tend to do... . Store them in an airtight, clean jar and keep them in a cool, dark storage place.

Fruit and veg. which have a high concentration of biogenic amines

Bananas, plums, walnuts, pears, raspberries, papaya and grapefruit contain other biogenic amines. These biogenic amines will be competing with the histamine because the diamine oxidase (DAO) is also responsible for their breakdown. The problem here will be that whatever reserves of diamine oxidase you may have will be exhausted very quickly. You will need individually to test out how high your tolerance of these different types of fruit and veg. is once you have gone through your elimination diet.

Fermented fruits and vegetables

Other foods containing high levels of histamine are soy products - such as soy sauce - vinegar, sauerkraut, all pickles and any foods that have been through a longer food manufacturing process. There are a number of food manufacturing processes that depend on the production of amines and similar chemicals for the flavour and nature of the food. Any process that requires microbial fermentation will result in the production of relatively high levels of amines, especially histamine. All types of vegetable products that have been produced by the fermentation process contain substantial levels of histamine.

Fruit and vegetables that liberate histamine stored in your body

Histamine releasers will lead to a spontaneous release of histamines stored in your mast cells. Tomatoes, as well as several citrus fruits such as pineapple and kiwi, are members of the group of histamine releasers. Experts seem to be at odds over whether strawberries are histamine releasers or just high in histamine due to the ripening process. Maybe it is both, who knows. What is clear, though, is that strawberries are a source of histamine and should therefore be avoided. Papaya, nuts, cocoa and chocolate are also members of this group. Other histamine releasers are buckwheat, sunflower seeds and mustard.

The way I tackled it was first to stick rigidly for the whole period of my elimination diet to all the veggies and fruits that were on the safe list. I stuck to what was fresh and safe as if my life depended on it... well, what other choice did I have?! At the same time I had to make sure that I was getting the right balance of minerals and vitamins. This is where the dieticians are able to give great advice. At the beginning it will be a very good idea to work out a diet plan together with the dietician. The more meticulous you are, the greater and faster the relief.

Smoothies

For those who are not affected by fructose malabsorption as well, smoothies are a great way of loading up with vitamins, especially when you're in a rush. If you do buy smoothies from shops where they make them fresh, make sure to check the precise ingredients. If you buy a pack, be sure to check the label. Many smoothies on the market which I have investigated will have bananas, amongst other culprits, in them. I once picked up a smoothie called "Blackcurrant & Apple" whose ingredients were meticulously listed as 495 blackcurrants, 4 apples and...here it comes...2 ½ bananas. Just enough to diminish the little DAO you might have in store. It's always a good idea to have a closer look at the full list of ingredients. On that note, looking at labels has become one of my favourite occupations in food shops. I do get the occasional strange looks, but you get used to it. Bananas are quite understandably used as a natural sweetener for smoothies, and also to give them texture. When you make a smoothie at home, you might like to add a teaspoon of honey or a little sugar in if you want to sweeten it up a bit.

Salad dressings

Another issue is the question of salad dressings. Since vinegar is one of the main components in today's standard salad dressings it seems quite difficult to make something that is tasty enough to eat, or so you might think. But, as always, there are alternatives. You should be able to tolerate small quantities of lemon. Lemon also has the enormous advantage of being a natural source of Vitamin C. Alternatively, you can make yourself a yogurt, sour cream or crème fraiche dressing with fresh herbs and a little garlic. Another really simple option is just to use olive oil, salt and pepper. I was made aware of this by a woman who has a combination of lactose intolerance, fructose malabsorption and histamine intolerance. She served it to her guests as part of a dinner and they all found it delicious. A combination of herbs and salad does not necessarily need an acidic component. This works very well with the mixed herb salads that you may be able to get from some shops.

I have noticed that in the HIT books which were written for the German language area, lemon is used throughout in the recipes. I do agree that if you want to add an acidic taste to any particular dish, then the best option will be to use either lemon, lemon zest, orange or orange zest according to tolerance, instead of vinegar, soy sauce and similar high histamine ingredients. The amounts of lemon juice tend to be minimal, especially when using it for the purpose of enhancing the taste of a dish, so it should normally not be anything to worry about.

18. BREAD & BAKING

Bread and its alternatives

Bread supplies you with starchy carbohydrates. It is one of the most important elements of your diet because bread, together with pasta, rice, whole grain products, cereals and potatoes will supply you with the energy you need. The body breaks carbohydrates down into the fuel you need for your cells and muscles.

Non-wheat pasta, rice, non-wheat whole grain bread or cookies made without yeast, cereals and potatoes of all types should not pose any problem for you. They are all said to have low histamine levels. In their original state only the whole grain products and cereals will contain some natural yeast. This is at such low levels that it should not pose a problem, except for those who are hyper-sensitive, which is apparently very rare.

This is not the case with ordinary bread. Most bread contains added yeast which contains very high levels of histamine. We consume an average of around 5 grams of yeast every day. This can lead to a severe reaction in people who are sensitive to this ingredient.

Those with intolerance to wheat, or coeliac disease, will have to work this additional factor in as well.

There are some products that have been marketed as yeast-free. However, they can turn out to be quite a disappointment. One of the main hitches is that other additives are included that just makes it all taste like a chemical brew. Apart from this, it may be only logical to suggest that bombarding the gut with more additives, even if different ones, may in the end turn out to be counterproductive and do more harm than good. So are these "health foods" really as healthy as they claim to be? Or is it just another marketing strategy to extract more money from those who are already desperate?

Some products are made without yeast but, if you examine the list of ingredients carefully, appear to contain soy flour, which is also not good for HITers.

Although they are difficult to locate in some places, it is worth while investigating all the soda breads. Breads that you can test individually are farls, Village Bakery Melmerby, Russian rye, French champagne,

Baltic rye, matzo crackers, oatcakes, corn cakes and rice cakes.

Wholegrain, wholemeal and brown bread give us energy and contain B vitamins, vitamin E, fibre and a wide range of minerals. White bread also contains a range of vitamins and minerals, but it has less fibre than wholegrain, wholemeal or brown bread.

The problem is that, as you can see above, bread is a really essential part of our diet and should not under any circumstance be cut out without having first talked to a professional dietician. They can tell you what alternative sources you can use to get the missing components back into the diet.

Bake your own bread

There is another, most delicious way of putting bread on the table. You can make your own, and with a little creativity it can be made in delicious varieties. Have a look at the recipe in the back of the book . The good thing about this bread is that you can make it at the weekend. It only takes up to two hours to make! You can eat some of it the same day, and you can freeze the rest in portions to supply you for the rest of the week. When you want to eat it, you can let it defrost for an hour, but I just stick it in the toaster and defrost it like that. Be careful not to defrost this bread more than once. It is best to stick to the principle "eat as fresh as possible".

Eggs

In baking you may often find that eggs are a major ingredient. The use of egg yolk is fine. The egg white is supposed to be the culprit. Egg white is said to have histamine releasing capacities, as well as using up a lot of Vitamin B6. Vitamin B6 in turn is a coenzyme, something like an assistant to DAO. When there is not enough of it around our DAO is missing some back-up. It has been suggested that HIT patients take Vitamin B6 supplements.

Gluten

Just to make things a little more interesting, it has been mentioned by Professor Maximillian Ledochowski in Innsbruck, Austria, that when gluten is broken down, some components can cause the release of histamine from mast cells. Mast cells are like little histamine storage cupboards, apart from their other functions. Patients with IBS, for example, seem to have more mast cells in the intestinal wall than others and are therefore likely to have a greater amount of histamine release when triggered, he says. Patients with HIT get symptoms if the amount of histamine floating around in the system can't be kept at bay because they can't produce enough DAO in time. It would be a good idea for both groups to try out whether reducing the gluten in their diet will do the trick. Wheat in general is under discussion as a culprit food for HIT patients.

Reintroduce bread if you can, as soon as you can!

Once you have finished your elimination diet it very important to see which bread and wheat products you can re-introduce. Cutting out this section of foods is in no way advisable unless you are allergic or are suffering from, for example, coeliac disease.

19.   THE PROBLEM WITH ALCOHOL!

Most of us love to go for a drink after work, relaxing after a hard day's slog or taking some time out at weekends. I used to have a glass or two of red wine with my meal quite frequently. That has changed completely. Here is a simplified rundown of why it is absolutely necessary to avoid any alcohol during the elimination diet, as well as to take a very cautious approach to re-introducing alcohol, and then only when the system can really handle it.

Wines, beers and spirits

Red wine is known to have some of the highest levels of histamine in alcoholic drinks and a bad reaction to small doses can be an indicator of HIT. White wines, including champagne, also have a relatively high histamine count. This, however, is generally much lower than in red wine, and can be much better tolerated, though only in small doses. In the category of beers, the top-fermented beers in their peak measurements have a lower histamine count than bottom-fermented beers. According to the current status, the beers can be placed somewhere between the red wines and the white wines with regard to their potential to aggravate any symptoms - which doesn't exactly make them a safe choice either. It has been said that spirits seem to give the least cause for complaint. But this is not the end of the story.

Have no illusions, alcohol is out

There are some other factors that need to be looked at to understand why alcohol needs to be avoided. You don't have to take my word for it. This is what the experts say:

"Alcohol enhances the effect of histamine and other biogenic amines, such as tyramine, by dilating (widening) vessels, changing the permeability of the intestinal wall and inhibiting the enzyme diamine oxidase.

Liquids also cause a higher local impact on the small intestine, which is the reason why the enzyme diamine oxidase is quickly exhausted.

Alcohol acts as a histamine liberator and therefore causes the release of the histamine that is located in the body's cells.

Acetaldehyde, a by-product of alcohol, is a histamine-releaser as well as an inhibitor of DAO.

Some alcoholic drinks, especially wine and beer, contain sulphite (recognisable on ingredient lists as E221-8) either as a by-product or as an additive. Sulphite is classed as another of the histamine-releasers. "

Basically this is the same effect as if you were gagging and tying up your DAO enzymes while bombarding them with a flood of histamine and Co., who, turned into well-trained thugs, pass by laughing their socks off at the victims who have been hamstrung by Mr. Acetaldehyde.

Being disciplined – saying no

After the diagnosis I had to come to the realisation that, at the start of my venture, alcohol in any form did not do me any good at all. This was quite a learning process. It was not just about giving up a habit. Abstaining from alcohol in a world where drinking booze is socially accepted, and sadly enough sometimes even expected, can have quite an impact on the pleasures of life. The best defence is to stay firm and don't give in to social pressures. But I must admit that by now, occasionally, I do have a little alcohol, in the form of a long drink based on spirits such as gin or vodka. Although this is said to be less harmful than many other alcoholic beverages, I do have to bear the consequences if I overstep my own tolerance limit – and those consequences are no pleasure at all – so I mainly stay off alcohol altogether.

What drinking alcohol means is that your ability to digest other foods that contain histamine will either be diminished or at least be severely impaired until your DAO count has been able to recover to some reasonable level. If you drink any alcohol at all, then it is best after a meal. Keep in the back of your mind that alcohol in larger quantities is bad for you anyway.

Non-alcoholic beverages

In comparison to alcoholic drinks there are only a few non-alcoholic beverages that you might have to avoid. Most of them should not be a problem. Watch out for sulphites, which are often used as antioxidants and preservatives in beverages. Some energy drinks are not suitable due to their theobromine content. Theobromine is a DAO blocker and can also be found in mate tea and cocoa products (e.g.chocolate)- see below. It is best to avoid them.

Water

Water contains no histamine. To keep yourself hydrated, start the day with a glass of water. It is easy to make it a habit as part of the morning routine.

Tea, coffee and cocoa

What proved even more difficult was to switch off my habit of drinking black (Indian) tea on a constant basis. I used to have at least four cups a day. The problem with tea, coffee and cocoa is that they contain caffeine, an alkaloid drug that has a stimulant action, particularly on the nervous system. Well, that's why we like to drink it. It is used to promote wakefulness and increase mental activity; it also possesses diuretic properties, and large doses may cause headaches. Caffeine is also often included in medicines with aspirin or codeine in order to counter their tendency to make you sleepy. Unfortunately, because of its stimulating properties, caffeine can also enhance any of the symptoms that are brought about by histamine intolerance.

In my quest to find out what theobromine is all about, a question frequently asked by other patients as well, I was given the following information from food scientist Ronke Shona: "Cocoa beans (Theobroma Cacao) naturally contain approximately 300 – 1200 mg/oz (that would be 10.6-42.4mg/g) of theobromine. Theobromines are naturally occurring alkaloids (methylxanthine) and the weaker relatives of caffeine.

Different chocolates contain different amounts theobromine:

Dark Chocolates – approximately 10g/kg

Milk Chocolates – approximately 1 – 5g/kg

Basically, the higher quality chocolates contain more theobromine than the lower quality varieties. At the end of processing from cocoa seeds, chocolates contain about 380 known chemicals, especially phenyl ethylamine (amphetamines). That is why it is known as a "Psychoactive Food". Being a psychoactive food, it triggers the release of histamine in non-mast cell locations such as the brain – hence the headaches/migraines - and enterochromaffin-like cells in the stomach – hence the cramps after eating cocoa/chocolate based products."

After your elimination diet you should be able to test out your individual threshold in combination with your other food intake. It is also a good idea to test out some 'decaf' tea or coffee. Or stick with herbal teas you find soothing.

Other hot beverages

In normal circumstances there should not be a problem with herbal teas or fruit teas without black tea or flavourings from fruits you need to avoid. You will need to test out which fruit teas you can handle. Since the fruit in the tea, yet again, has gone through a manufacturing process, fermentation might pose a problem, although the likelihood is low. If you have a garden, it might be a good idea to grow a pot of mint. Better not put it straight in the earth though. Mint spreads uncontrollably if not confined to a pot. Take a bunch of mint leaves, scrunch them up a little bit with a pestle and mortar and stuff it all into a cup or tea-glass with a little sugar. Pour some hot water over it and let it infuse. It's the closest you can get to the real thing. Whole nations swear by hot, sweet mint tea, so why not take a leaf out of their book.

Juices and soft-drinks

Obviously avoid anything that is a chemical brew. Some soft drinks may contain coffee or benzoates, so have a good look at the label before you buy. Fruit juices are fine as long as you exclude the ones on the list of fruits you need to avoid, such as tomato juice, strawberry, kiwi, pineapple etc. The same applies to yoghurt drinks, milkshakes and smoothies (see above). If you have had to exclude some of your favourites, you can test them out after your elimination diet.

20.   PHARMACEUTICALS, FOOD ADDITIVES, E-NUMBERS AND OTHER CULPRITS

An important word of caution first of all. If you are a patient under medication and may have discovered that you are taking any of the substances mentioned below you must first consult with your GP or medical consultant on what to do next before you change anything at all. You must first consult your doctor or specialist before you decide to stop taking any medication or change the drug, otherwise you may do yourself harm. Your doctor should know how to verify if a certain drug may harm you more than it does you good. If in doubt, bring it to their attention and discuss any possible side effects, or get a referral to a specialist.

Substances in medications that can affect the enzyme diamine oxidase negatively

Prof. Dr. med. Ralf Bauer, specialist for skin and venereal disease and doctor of venereology at the University Clinic in Bonn's dermatological department clinic and polyclinic, has compiled a list of 93 substances that can influence the activity of DAO. This list was published in a book entitled "Histamin-Intoleranz, Histamin und Seekrankheit" by Prof. Reinhart Jarisch of the Allergy Centre Floridsdorf in Vienna. This book is currently only available in German (2010). Updates on the availability of this list in the English language area will be made known on the website www.histamineintolerance.org.uk. The substances on the list should ideally be taken into consideration when a choice is made regarding the patient's medication and its suitability, so that any additional triggering of Histamine Intolerance symptoms can be avoided.

The following are examples of common pharmaceutical ingredients that can possibly have a debilitating effect on DAO or release histamine in individual cases. This may just look like a list of long, unpronounceable names, but they are important if you want to check on the packaging whether it has been prescribed for you or ask a doctor in hospital if it is being used. This list is intended to help you and your doctor and, as emphasized above, never stop taking your prescribed medicine without first consulting your doctor:

Examples of substances and what they are intended for:

Acetylcysteine – Treatment with intravenous acetylcysteine is commonly used in the United Kingdom in patients with acetaminophen (paracetamol) poisoning. Some medication with this ingredient is used to prevent kidney damage that is a risk when contrast agent is used to make something show up during an examination.

Ambroxol – Can be used as part of therapy for bronchitis.

Aminophylline - is widely used to dilate the air passages in the treatment of severe asthma and some cases of chronic obstructive pulmonary diseases. Some medication with this ingredient is used in conditions where the airways contract, such as asthma or chronic obstructive pulmonary disease (COPD, eg emphysema and chronic bronchitis), where it is difficult to breathe in or out.

Amitriptyline – This drug acts on nerve cells in the brain and is an antidepressant that has a mild tranquilising effect; it may be used to treat bedwetting in children.

Cimetidine - An antihistamine (H2 antagonist) that is used to treat ulcers and duodenal ulcers, gastroesophagal reflux disease and other digestive disorders.

Chloroquine – is a drug used principally in the treatment and prevention of benign malarias but also occasionally in the treatment of rheumatoid arthritis and lupus erythematosus.

Clavulanic acid – A drug that is mainly used in connection with bacterial infections.

Isoniazide – is a drug used in the treatment of tuberculosis. It is normally used in combination with other drugs.

Metamizole - is a non-steroidal anti-inflammatory drug (NSAID), commonly used in the past as a powerful painkiller and fever reducer. NSAIDs are commonly used during and after operations.

Metoclopramide – is a drug used to treat nausea and vomiting, particularly when associated with gastrointestinal disorders.

Propafenone – is used to treat irregular heart beat (arrhythmias).

Verapamil - is used in treatment of essential hypertension, angina and arrhythmia.

Histamine liberators/releasers

Narcotics such as codeine and morphine have been proven to have a histamine releasing effect. This also applies to contrast agents. Scientists have come to the conclusion that because an adverse reaction to contrast agents can be almost completely suppressed by anti-histamines (such as H1 and H2 receptor blockers) it is an indication that the main reason for contrast agent intolerance is the increased histamine release or the inability of the person to break down the excess of liberated histamines.

The fear factor and coping with stress

Another aspect that needs to be taken into account is that a person in a stressful situation or also in fear of an anticipated situation will be releasing a higher amount of histamine into the system. This is normally a positive reaction, part of the body's natural defences, but for an HIT sufferer this may mean extra problems and a higher likelihood of experiencing those undesirable symptoms. Everybody has their own way of dealing with stress. There are countless techniques out there. The best strategy here is to find whatever suits you best as an individual. Something you can do at home, or together with others, be it yoga, tai chi, going for walks with your dog, breathing exercises or autogenic training, for example. Try to give yourself some downtime once a day, especially before you go to sleep. It will be in your sleep when histamine activity in the brain goes down. Histamine is also responsible for the regulation of your sleep-wake rhythm. Your histamine-level drops towards zero when you are asleep.

Histamine Intolerance and motion sickness

In a very complex discussion by the Viennese Professor and Head of the Allergy Centre in Vienna, Reinhart Jarisch, it has been suggested that the primary cause of motion sickness is histamine. Should this statement be true, then this will have great relevance for HIT sufferers and their travel plans. There are several remedies that have been discussed, and the overall placebo rate of the available medications has been given as an average of 30 percent. In the study the antihistamine cinnarizine, used for tinnitus, vertigo and travel sickness, seems to be what works best, although it may have side effects such as drowsiness, tremors and rigidity. As part of overcoming motion sickness he suggests remaining in the middle of the ship or other vehicle where there is the least possible movement and looking in the direction in which you are travelling, since optical impulses have a certain amount of influence in motion sickness. A further approach is to eat foods that are fresh and low in histamine. The person can also opt to take a dose of 2 grams Vitamin C in advance, and then, at the onset of feeling motion-sick, take a high dose of 500mg Vitamin C in the form of chewable tablets, since Vitamin C assists the degradation of histamine. As mentioned above, there is the additional option of finding a relatively quiet place to relax and if possible go to sleep.

This may be an explanation for why I myself get sea-sick on smaller vessels even when there is little swell. I was on a filming trip in Turkey and had forgotten all about this theory. We were probably only 10 minutes into the trip when the vessel stopped so that we could film. It was swaying a little from side to side. We had to turn the vessel so that it would be in the right place to film a scene with the archaeologist and TV presenter rowing a boat. During this whole procedure I started to feel quite unwell and the fumes of the engine exhaust just made it worse. I sat down. That did not help. I asked the captain for a place to lie down in the fresh air, which was immediately provided. It did not take long until my body just automatically shut down and I went to sleep. I didn't even realise when we returned to port although the motor, when running, was really loud. I must have slept for at least an hour. Just as we landed I was woken up by my colleagues, who were naturally a little concerned but had a little chuckle once they saw that I was fine. The most interesting thing about this episode is that I felt absolutely fine when I woke up. It was almost as if nothing had ever happened. Only later did I make a connection. The cause of this may be subject to discussion in the future and I can certainly not say for sure that my motion sickness was caused by my histamine intolerance. The facts are that I have histamine intolerance, I got sea-sick, I went to sleep, and it worked.

So what does all this mean for the patient?

This is a short extract of what Prof. Reinhard Jarisch says in his book about histamine intolerance and the following situations:

Concerning contrast agents:

A patient with histamine intolerance (HIT) will need to inform their doctor of their condition.

It is sensible to follow a histamine-free diet 24 hours before the examination in order to minimise a high exposure to histamine.

For the radiologist it means that patients who possess a higher degree of risk should be given pre-medication (H1 or H2 receptor blockers) as a precautionary measure.

Concerning surgery, including going to the dentist:

He discusses the combination of fear and pain, which naturally results in the increased release of histamines by the body. Incisions by scalpels have the same effect. He states that the release of histamines is increased by dramatic circumstances, meaning that every blow to the body, every accident, every injury caused by an accident, but also the cut of a scalpel at the beginning of an operative procedure will lead to the release of histamine. He points out that anaesthetists are confronted over and over again with incidents of falling blood pressure and breathing problems in patients. Patients at the dentist frequently experience a fall in blood pressure, which is often blamed on the local anaesthetic although allergic reactions to local anaesthetics are very rare.

He therefore advises the doctors responsible not only to establish if the patient has any allergies, but also to see if there is a dysfunction in the degradation of histamines. The patient could be supported by administering antihistamines in the form of H1 receptor blockers.

The patient can contribute by going on a histamine-free diet 24 hours before the surgery or before going to the dentist, as well as to try to conquer their fear with the likes of autogenic training.

Food at hospitals

Some patients may be lucky enough to end up in a hospital that has a good quality of service as well as food. But many of us know only too well what food can be like in these institutions and patients have even been known to refuse to eat it. A journalist in the UK, calling himself Traction Man in his internet blog, who has been in and out of hospital in the UK since August 2009, has even created a page where he asks viewers to identify what is on his plate. He says that people justifiably cannot guess what some of the meals are. When looking at the pictures it is not surprising. Most unbelievable of all is that fast food and coffee chains are being allowed to open up outlets in hospitals, the very places where fast food and pre-prepared food should be the last thing a patient should be offered. For the HIT patient this constitutes extra pitfalls. HITers need to be supplied with low histamine food otherwise the hospitals actually risk harming the patient. This diet choice is not made available in most institutions, due to their lack of knowledge or straightforward ignorance of this subject. At the moment the only way to get fresh meals in many places is to rely on family and friends who can cook a proper meal and bring it in. Needless to say, this is a totally unsatisfactory solution. A lot of information campaigning will need to be done here.

Thoughts for the future – the HIT pass

Maybe sometime in the future there will be some kind of pass for people who have been positively diagnosed with HIT. A pass that is similar to that of diabetes patients. It would be very helpful to have such a pass for those who need to go for treatments and surgery in hospital, or when the patient has to have contrast agents administered, for example, or in the case of an accident where the patient is in no condition to inform those treating them. It would be even better if everyone concerned in treatment were equipped with the information about the above substances, so that they can prescribe patients the right medication in the first place.

Food additives

Another mode of histamine release associated with food is suggested by research into the mechanisms of intolerance associated with food additives. It is suspected that Azo (nitrogen-containing) food dyes such as tartrazine and preservatives such as benzoates, sorbates and possibly sulphites (often added to red wines) release histamine, though it is not yet known precisely how. Additional substances that can act as histamine releasers are, for example, glutamate and nitrite, used to enhance the taste and appearance of food.

E-numbers to avoid

Examples of additives which are under discussion and should at least be avoided during the elimination diet, because they are suspected of stimulating the white blood cells to release histamine are:

Food colourings (E100-104, 120, 123, 127,128,131,132)

Sorbates (200 – 203)

Benzoates and PHB-Ester (E210-219)

Sulphites (E220 - 228)

Glutamate (E620-625)

So take a good look at the labels (even if it means putting on your reading glasses in public to decipher the small print, or even getting out a magnifying glass) and put anything with any of these ingredients right back on the shelf! Don't forget, it all depends on your personal threshold. Better still, wherever possible, cook it yourself from fresh where possible. Then you know exactly what is in it. If I can do it, so can you!

List of additives that need to be avoided

Food colours and dyes:

E 100 Curcumin - One of the components of tumeric (could be called the active ingredient), alongside Demethoxy-curcumin and Bisdemethoxy-curcumin. Powerful anti-inflammatory, anti-oxidant, antiviral and anti-fungal. Uses: mustard, margarine, processed cheese, cakes, soft drinks, curry powder.

E 101 Lactoflavin, Riboflavin - Vitamin B2; is a natural component of some foods. It is required by all flavoproteins (proteins that contain a nucleic acid derivative of riboflavin). Important in a wide variety of cellular processes. Naturally present in many foods, but commercially prepared from yeast. Uses: Baby foods, pasta, breakfast cereals, pasta sauces, processed cheese. Intake isn't a problem since it is continuously excreted in urine (deficiency is more likely than overdose).

E 101a Riboflavin-5'-phosphate; Lactoflavin phosphate ester. More expensive, but soluble form of E101.

E 102 Tartrazine – lemon yellow food dye. It's a synthetic "Azo Dye". Not to be used by asthmatics and people intolerant to aspirin. Banned in Norway and Austria (commonly used in the UK). Reactions include; indigestion and immunological reactions – blurred vision, sleep disturbances, general weakness, itching and anxiety.

E 104 Quinoline - Yellow – synthetic dull yellow or greenish yellow food dye. It's a synthetic coal tar dye. Banned in Australia, Japan, Norway and USA (believed to cause dermatitis). Known histamine liberator. Uses: cough sweets, scotch eggs, smoked haddock.

E 120 Cochineal, carminic acid, carmines – food dye for scarlet, orange or red tinted colours. Crimson coloured dye which is derived from the insect Cochineal. Reactions include; mild cases of hives, atrial fibrillation and anaphylactic shock, asthma. Uses: alcoholic drinks (red wine), meat, sausages, processed poultry.

E 123 Amaranth – synthetic deep red food dye frequently in wine, spirits and fish roe. Purplish-red synthetic coal tar (azo dye), derived from small herbaceous plants. Banned in Norway, USA, Russia and Austria. Restricted use in France and Italy (for caviar only). Reactions include; nettle rash, asthma and eczema. Cancerous (?). Proven birth deformities in clinical animal testing. Uses: ice creams, gravy granules, jams, jellies, prawns, cake mixes, soups and trifles.

E 127 Erythrosine – Cherry-pink/red synthetic coal tar dye. Banned in Norway and USA. Reactions include; photosensitivity in some people. Uses: tinned cherries, canned fruit, custard mix, biscuits, chocolates, salmon spread, stuffed olives, scotch eggs.

E 128 Red 2G – Synthetic red azo dye. Banned in Australia, Austria, Canada, Japan, Norway, Sweden, Malaysia, Ireland, Israel and Greece. Concerns include; Red 2G can be converted into "aniline" (toxic compound). Red 2G may interfere with blood haemoglobin as well as being cancerous. Uses: cooked meat products, sausages, jams.

E 131 Patent blue V – Dark bluish-violet synthetic coal tar dye. Banned in Australia, USA and Norway. Reactions include; skin sensitivity, nausea, hypotension (low blood pressure), tremors, breathing difficulties, anaphylactic shock. Uses: scotch eggs, some jelly sweets. Also used in dental tablets to identify plaque.

E 132 Indigotine; Indigo Carmine – Blue synthetic coal tar dye. Naturally present in the shrub called Indigofertinctoria. Banned in Norway. Reactions include; high blood pressure breathing difficulties, skin sensitivity. Also used for pharmaceuticals.

Preservative agents:

E 200 Sorbic acid – not to be confused with ascorbic acid (Vit C)! It isolated from unripe Rowan berries (Sorbus Aucuparia). White crystalline solid. Can be manufactured synthetically from the toxic, colourless gas ketene. Antimicrobial (prevents growth of mould, yeast and fungi). Banned in Australia. Reactions; possible skin irritant. Uses: frozen pizzas, sweet yoghurt, fruit salads, cider, dessert sauces, beverage.

E 201 Sodium sorbate – It's a sodium salt of sorbic acid (E200). Prepared by the neutralisation of sorbic acid. Used in the same range of products as sorbic acid.

E 202 Potassium sorbate – It's a potassium salt of sorbic acid, made by the neutralisation of sorbic acid. Used in the same range of products as sorbic acid. Also used in wines as stabiliser and frequently in foods such as milk products and bakery.

E 203 Calcium sorbate – It's a calcium salt of sorbic acid, made by the neutralisation of sorbic acid. It is used in a diverse range of products.

E 210 Benzoic acid – mould, yeast and bacteria inhibitor used in acidic foods. Colourless crystalline organic compound, synthetically made by the oxidisation of benzene with concentrated sulphuric acid or carbon dioxide in the presence of catalyst. Naturally occurring in many edible berries, fruits and vegetables. Resin is exuded by trees native to Asia. Reactions include; gastric irritation and asthma. Also reputed to cause some neurological disorders. Uses: beer, coffee essence, fruit juices, jam, margarine, pickles ...

E 211 Sodium benzoate – is often added to vinegars, carbonated drinks, condiments and cough syrups. Made by neutralisation of sodium hydroxide with benzoic acid. Antibacterial and antifungal under acidic conditions. Reactions include; asthma, aspirin sensitivity. Uses: Barbecue sauce, caviar, cheese, prawns, preserves, soy sauce, milk ...

E 212 Potassium benzoate – frequently added to fruit juices and soft drinks. Antibacterial and antifungal properties. Reactions include; asthma, urticaria (skin disease), mild irritation to the skin, eyes and mucus membranes. Uses: margarine, pickled cucumber, pineapple juice, table olives...

E 213 Calcium benzoate – preservative for many drinks, diet products, cereals and meat products. Colourless white crystals or powder. Naturally occurs in fruits, especially berries as well as cinnamon, cloves and mushrooms. As a result of fermentation, also occurs naturally in some dairy products. Reactions include; asthma, hay fever, hives, rashes, headaches, intestine upset.

E 214 Ethyl p-hydroxybenzoate – preservative for many fruit products including jams and salad cream. Antimicrobial and antifungal. Not effective against bacteria. Reactions include; may cause pseudo-allergic reactions. Banned in France and Australia.

E 215 Sodium ethyl p-hydroxybenzoate, sodium salt – banned in some countries as one of the cancerous food additives. Similar to E214. Also banned in France and Australia. Well-known histamine liberator.

E 216 Propyl p-hydroxybenzoate – added to cereals, snacks, pâté and confectionary. Occurs naturally in many plants and some insects. Banned in France and Australia. Histamine liberator. Reactions same as E214. Uses: beverages, candy, artificially sweetened jellies and preserves…..

E 217 Sodium propyl para-hydroxybenzoate – banned in some countries as one of the cancerous food additives. Antimicrobial preservative. Banned in France and Australia due to cancer links.

E 218 Methyl p-hydroxybenzoate – widely used preservative against yeast and fungi. Banned in France and Australia. Main reaction is skin irritation. Uses: alcoholic drinks, ice cream, baked goods, medicine.

E 219 Sodium methyl p-hydroxybenzoate – Banned in France and Australia.

E 220 Sulphur dioxide – often used as bleaching agent in flour, as stabiliser of foods including Vitamin C, and is known to contribute to intestinal diseases. Colourless toxic gas. Derived from coal tar. Banned for use on raw fruits and vegetables in the USA. Used to prevent enzymatic spoilage. Antibacterial. Reactions include; Asthma, kidney failure, destroys vitamins B1 and E, gastrointestinal disturbances. Uses: used in a broad range of acidic products.

E 221 Sodium sulphite – used as stabiliser or oxidising and bleaching agent and can for instance be found in products with egg yolk, salads and bread, wine-making and processed foods. White non-stable powder. Reactions are the same as E220.

E 222 Sodium hydrogen sulphite – preservative and bleaching agent also found in preserved onions, alcoholic beverages, dairy products, fruit juices and mashed potato

E 223 Sodium metabisulphite – found in preserved onions, alcoholic beverages, bakery products, fruit juices and potato products.

E 224 Potassium metabisulphite – often added to preserved onions, wine, preserved fruits, shellfish and more.

E 226 Calcium sulphite – often used as bleaching agent in sugar production and is known to increase the firmness of canned vegetables (due to calcium). It is banned in the USA.

E 227 Calcium hydrogen sulphite – Is used in beer production and is known to increase the firmness of canned vegetables (due to calcium)

E 228 Potassium hydrogen sulphite – also used for acid preserved fruits and in wines

Flavour Enhancers:

E 620 Glutamic acid – glutamic acid and glutamates are known for the umami taste enhancement and are found in many different products. Glutamates are present in high concentrations in ripened cheese, tomatoes and sardines. It's a natural amino acid. Commercially prepared from molasses by bacterial fermentation. Not suitable for consumption by children. There is no clear scientific relation with the intake of MSG.

E 621 Monosodium glutamate – (see above)

E 622 Monopotassium glutamate – (see above)

E 623 Calcium diglutamate – (see above) frequently used in low-salt products

E 624 Monoammonium glutamate – (see above)

E 625 Magnesium diglutamate – Hardly used, only in low sodium meat products

21. FOOD LISTS AND SUPPLEMENTS

A low-histamine diet needs to be observed for 3-4 weeks

The Food List

The most important thing to remember is to eat foods that are low in histamine, according to your threshold.

Here are some general pointers:

Avoid or reduce eating canned food and ready meals

Avoid or reduce eating ripened and fermented foods (older cheeses, alcoholic drinks, products with yeast, older fish...)

Levels of histamine in foods can vary! This depends on how ripe, how matured, or how hygienic a product is – or how much it has fermented.

Only buy and eat products that are as fresh as possible.

Don't leave foods like animal products, or anything perishable, to linger outside the fridge.

Keep your kitchen clean – without getting paranoid.

Every person has their own threshold; you will need to find yours. Talk to a dietician about working out a balanced diet.

Learn to cook! Its loads of fun once you get into it. ;-)

Please be aware that, because of any other food intolerances or cross-allergies that may also be present, the low-histamine content of a particular foodstuff alone says nothing definite about whether or not the patient can tolerate it.

Foods that have lower histamine levels and are thus to be preferred:

- Fresh meat (fresh, cooled, frozen)

- Freshly caught fish

- Chicken (skinned, fresh – chicken tends to deteriorate quickly, so make sure it is fresh!)

- Egg yolk

- Fresh fruit: apple, apricot, blueberry, cranberries (lingonberries), khaki, litchi, mango, melon, red currants

- Fresh vegetables: asparagus, beetroot, bell peppers (not chillies!), broccoli, cabbage, carrot, corn, cucumber, garlic, lamb's lettuce, lettuce, onion, potatoes, pumpkin, radishes, rhubarb

- Grains, pasta: spelt-, corn-, rice noodles; yeast-free rye bread; corn-, rice crisp bread; rice; rolled/porridge oats, oat flakes; puffed rice crackers; corn-, rice-, millet flower.

- Fresh milk and milk products

- Substitutes for milk (especially for those with additional lactose intolerance): rice-, oat-, coconut milk

- Cream cheese

- All fruit juices without citrus fruits and/or juices without added tomato, all vegetable juices (except Sauerkraut)

- Herbal teas (except those mentioned below)

Foods that have higher levels of histamine:

- Alcohol, especially beer and wine

- Pickled or canned foods

- Cheese: especially mature cheese – the more mature the more histamine it contains

- Smoked meats, smoked ham and Salami

- Most fish products (all shellfish), especially canned fish

- Beans and pulses (especially chickpeas, soy beans, also peanuts)

- Soy products (soy milk, soy cream, tofu, soy sauces, ...)

- Sauerkraut or other pickled foods

- Some fruits (aubergines, bananas, kiwi, oranges, pears, strawberries)

- Nuts, walnuts, cashew nuts

- Chocolate, cocoa, salty snacks, sweets with preservatives and artificial colourings

- Products made from wheat

- Vinegar

- Yeast

- Ready meals

- Black tea

Foods that release histamine (histamine releasers)

- Citrus fruits
- Cocoa and chocolate
- Kiwi
- Lemon
- Lime
- Nuts
- Papaya
- Pineapple
- Plums
- Pulses
- Raspberries
- Strawberries
- Tomatoes
- Wheat germ
- Additives: Benzoate, Food dyes, Glutamate, Nitrites, Sulphites

Foods that block the diamine oxidase (DAO) enzyme:

- Alcohol

- Black tea

- Cocoa

- Energy drinks (component theobromine blocks the DAO)

- Green tea

- Mate tea

Debatable:

- Cherries

- Courgette

- Egg white

- Leek

- Yoghurt

An elimination diet normally takes around 4 weeks. By then you should feel a lot better – then it is time to figure out your personal threshold.

Sources include:

NMI-Portal, www.Nahrungsmittel-Intoleranz.com

Maintz L, Noval N: Histamine and histamine intolerance, American Journal of Clinical Nutrition 2007

Jarisch, R. "Histaminunverträglichkeit", Thieme Verlag, 2nd Edition

A few words on vitamins and other supplements:

The following supplements have been suggested. It is better, however, to try to ingest these by eating foods that contain them rather than popping pills. Only resort to taking supplements when absolutely necessary and in accordance with your doctor's advice or that of a dietician:

Vitamin C: lowers the histamine level in the blood

Vitamin B6: is an important co-factor of the enzyme diamine oxidase and its activity

Calcium: reduces the development of wheals and flushing of the skin

Zinc: has anti-allergic and anti-inflammatory properties and constrains histamine release

Copper: is able to elevate the plasma level of DAO slightly

Magnesium: a Magnesium deficit lowers the allergic reaction threshold

Manganese: elevates diamine oxidase activity

Vitamin B1

Vitamin B12

Folic Acid

Anti-histamines (H1 and H2 receptor blockers) are able to block the effects of histamine, but remember they are just suppressing the symptoms, not tackling the underlying cause.

DAO enzyme supplements (up to 3 capsules a day) have been suggested (see discussion above).

Since anti-histamines and DAO-supplements are not the solution, it is advisable to adjust the diet to the patient's needs with the help of a qualified dietician.

Vitamin C

Higher concentrations of Vitamin C can generally be found in vegetables and fruits. Research results concerning contents of Vitamin C vary slightly, but are mostly similar. Due to the varying amounts, this is an approximate list, where fruits and vegetables with higher amounts are listed first. Any fruits and vegetables not represented in this list also contain Vitamin C and are valuable as part of a balanced diet, so there is no reason to exclude them. Although the potato is further down on the list, it is worth mentioning that since we do consume large amounts of this vegetable it is one of the most important sources of Vitamin C:

Blackcurrant	Cauliflower	Watermelon
Red pepper	Garlic	Carrot
Parsley	Cabbage	Cherry
Broccoli	Lime	Peach
Loganberry	Mango	Apple
Red currant	Potato	Asparagus
Brussels sprouts	Melon	Beetroot
Lychee	Blueberry	Pear
Elderberry	Grape	Lettuce
Lemon	Apricot	Cucumber
Melon	Plum	Fig

In the year 2009 the recommendations RDA for daily Vitamin C intake for healthy adults vary from country to country, but can generally be found in the region of 60mg/day to 110mg/day for healthy adults. Saturation level of vitamin C in the blood is reported to have been reached at 400mg/day, but is under discussion. Some believe this is too low and there is some ferocious discussion going on in the scientific community concerning this issue.

Vitamin C and DAO

Vitamin C is water soluble and has several functions. One of these functions is to help certain enzymes do the work they need to do. With regard to the relationship between diamine oxidase and Vitamin C, it appears to have been confirmed that the vitamin can chemically deactivate histamine and help with breaking down histamine.

The main source of Vitamin C in many countries diet is potatoes.

Vitamin C levels deteriorate in foods, depending on length of storage as well as the influence of temperature, oxygen supply and light. They are also reduced through the cooking process, so go easy on vegetables and fruits when you cook them.

Vitamin B6 (Pyridoxine, pyridoxal, pyridoxamine) and DAO

Vitamin B6 co-enzymes play an important role in amino acid metabolism. The daily intake is proportional to the protein intake, because proteins are composed of amino acids. It also plays a role in the production of red blood cells. Diamine oxidase has been found to be a Vitamin B6 dependent enzyme. It requires riboflavin, zinc and magnesium to fulfill its functions.

The RDA for vitamin B6 is 0.16mg/g protein. That means the average necessary intake is 2.0 mg/day for men and about 1.6 mg/day for women.

You should be able to get the amount you need by eating a varied and balanced diet. But if you decide to take vitamin B6 supplements it's important not to take too much because this could be harmful.

The UK's Food Standards Agency advises against taking more than 10 mg of vitamin B6 supplements a day. But you should continue taking a higher dose if this is under medical advice.

Sources of Vitamin B6 are mainly found in meat, fish and poultry. Other sources are bread, whole cereals (such as oatmeal and rice), eggs, vegetables, milk and potatoes and purple fruit.

Important last word

The information provided in this book is definitely not intended for use as part of self diagnosis or a self-constructed dietary plan. The lists are not exhaustive! It is by no means an alternative option to visiting your GP, a qualified nutritionist or a dietician.

You must not use the information in this book as a means of self-diagnosis otherwise you risk doing yourself serious harm.

22. RECIPES

Breakfast

Crispy oat and coconut with yoghurt and berry sauce

4 servings

2 tbsp honey

60g porridge oats

60g flaked almonds

20g desiccated coconut

200g berries (e.g. blueberries or red currants or blackcurrants...)

1 tbsp caster sugar

1-2 tbsp lemon juice

400g natural yoghurt of your preference

Put the honey, oats, almonds and coconut into a frying pan on a low to medium heat. Let the ingredients blend together and let them cook until they brown slightly. Be careful not to let them burn, so keep stirring every now and then. Pour the mixture onto some baking parchment on a flat surface, and let it cool down.

While your mix is cooling down, put two thirds of your choice of berries in the pan together with the caster sugar and lemon juice. Bring to the boil and then let it simmer on a really low heat for 5-10 minutes. The berries don't need to be cooked to a pulp. Take the pan off the heat and add the rest of the berries. Stir. Let this mixture cool down as well.

Once everything is cooled down to your liking, pour the berry mix into a bowl. Then evenly spread the yoghurt over the berry sauce - this works very well with Greek yoghurt, but you can use any kind of yoghurt you like. Then spread the oat-coconut mix on top. Ready to eat!

Spanish potato omelette

4 servings

4 tbsp olive oil

6 large eggs

400g waxy potatoes, peeled and diced into ½ cm cubes

1 medium (approx.125g) cour-gette (zucchini), diced in ½ cm cubes

1 bell pepper, similarly diced

1 onion, similarly diced

1 clove garlic, finely chopped (optional)

50g Gouda cheese, grated

Parsley, finely chopped

Salt and freshly ground pepper

Blanch the potatoes in boiling salted water for around 3 minutes. Meanwhile prepare the courgette, bell pepper, on-ion and garlic.

Heat half of the oil in a large frying pan and fry the onion until transparent, but not yet browned. Add the courgette and red pepper and fry for 3 minutes, add the garlic, continue to fry for another 2 minutes, then place the mixture in a bowl and put to aside.

Heat the remaining oil in the frying pan, add the potatoes and fry for another 3 minutes or until they are just starting to turn brown. Add the prepared onion and red pepper mixture and stir.

Beat the eggs in a bowl, add parsley as well as seasoning and stir in the grated cheese. Reduce the heat to low and pour the eggs evenly over the mixture in the frying pan. Cover and cook for 10 min-utes or until the eggs are set. Slide the omelette onto a plate, cut into 4 equal slices and serve.

Mango smoothie

4 servings

2 ripe mangos

300g yoghurt, chilled

600ml full milk, chilled

2 - 4 tsp honey

10 cardamom pods, seeds only

Peel the mango with a sharp knife and then continue to cut the flesh off the stone. Chop the mango flesh into chunks to fit into the blender and blend until smooth.

Add all of the honey, yoghurt and the milk and continue to blend until it is all well mixed. Stir in the cardamom seeds.

Pour into cold glasses and it is ready to serve.

Smoothies are a great way of getting some vitamins inside of you. There are many different versions out there of different combinations of fruit and here you can really go to town with your experimenting. Apart from fruit of your choice you can add milk and/or yoghurt. You can also add spices that you feel comfortable using, like cinnamon, cardamom or ginger. You can also add mint or a little fresh ginger where you find it fitting. Sweeteners such as maple syrup or honey are another option, and some people even add oats or milled oats, milled linseed and similar ingredients.

Pancakes with triple fruit compote

4 servings

For the batter:

125g flour or rice flour

2 eggs

125ml milk

125ml single or whipping cream

Zest of ½ lemon

A pinch of salt

1tsp butter or vegetable oil

Compote see next page

Bring a little water to the boil in a saucepan. Add the sugar, cinnamon stick, apple and pear pieces and cook gently for 10 minutes.

Then add the lemon zest and the plum chunks and cook for another 10 to 15 minutes on a low heat or until tender. After cooking remove the cinnamon stick.

For the pancake batter sift the flour and a pinch of salt into a large bowl. Whisk together the milk and cream with the eggs and lemon zest in a jug. Pour the mixture into the bowl with the dry ingredients and whisk until the batter is smooth.

Get the pan really hot and then turn down to a medium heat. Add a tiny bit of butter or vegetable oil. With a large ladle pour some batter into the pan and turn it so that the batter covers the whole flat surface. Wait around 2 minutes until the batter starts to loosen from the pan. With the help of a palette knife have a little peak at the bottom of the pancake and see if it has started to brown. If it has, then flip the pancake onto the other side and cook for another minute. Transfer the pancake to a plate and keep warm. Repeat the process until you have used up all the batter.

For the compote:

1 eating apple, peeled, cored and cut into large chunks

2 pears, peeled, cored and cut into large chunks

3 plums, washed and stoned, and cut into large chunks

1 cinnamon stick, approx 3-4 cm length

Zest of ½ lemon

2-3 tbsp sugar

Put each pancake on a warmed plate (in the oven at lowest temperature). Put 2-3 tablespoons of compote on one half of the pancake and fold over the other half. Sprinkle with some icing sugar. Ready.

If you are using rice flour then you will need to be a little more careful with turning the pancakes over as they tend to break. (If that happens, just mix the pancake bits with the compote and give it another name!) Otherwise they are just as delicious as pancakes made with any other kind of flour. Rice flour pancakes also tend to be a little lighter than others.

You can also have the compote as a snack on its own any time of day.

Ham, cheese and basil on crisp-bread

4 servings

4 pieces crisp-bread

100g mild cheese (cheddar, Gouda), grated

100g cooked ham, in slices

4 fresh basil leaves, cut into strips

Preheat the oven to 200 C.

Place a slice of ham on each crisp-bread. Sprinkle grated cheese on top and bake in the oven for 5-7 minutes or until the cheese has started to brown.

Sprinkle each piece with basil strips and serve immediately.

Soups & Salads

Simple chicken stock

This is a recipe for simple and fast stock. The difference between this one and the advanced version is that it does not have as intense a flavour, but it is certainly a good alternative for those who have little time to spare. If you have some left over at the end you can freeze it after straining through a sieve and use it for another dish in future.

1litre water

300g chicken breast or equivalent

1 onion, chopped into large chunks

2 carrots, peeled and chop into 1 cm size chunks

1-2 stems celery, chopped into 1 cm size chunks

A handful of parsley, with stems and all

1 clove

1 bay leaf

Salt

Bring the water to the boil in a large saucepan. Meanwhile, wash and prepare all the vegetables and set aside.

Cut the chicken into large chunks.

Put the chicken pieces into the boiling water and bring back to the boil. If you are using chicken on the bone, and some froth appears on the surface of the water after a little while, then skim it off with a spoon. This normally happens when you use meat on the bone, which makes the stock even tastier.

Now add the rest of the ingredients above and put a lid on. Leave to simmer for 35 – 45 minutes. Make sure that it is not cooking too rapidly, just slightly simmering.

Pour the stock through a sieve and it will be ready to use or, after it has cooled down, can be frozen for future use.

You can use the vegetables and the meat from the chicken for any further cooking as well. See the chicken fricassee recipe for example.

Vegetable stock

200g leek, roughly chopped in 1/2cm rounds

300g carrot, roughly chopped as above

1 parsnip, roughly chopped as above

2 celery stalks, roughly chopped in 1cm lengths

1 onion, chopped to resembles size of the above

Handful parsley, with stalks

1 leaf lovage (if you can find any – optional)

1 bay leaf

A few peppercorns

1,5 – 2 litres water

Chop the leek, carrot, parsnip, celery and onion to approximately the same size. Wash the herbs. Put all the ingredients and water into a large thick-bottomed pan. Bring to the boil, cover and let it simmer lightly on a low heat for 20 to 25 minutes.

Pour the liquid through a sieve into a bowl. At this point you can season with salt and use it for a recipe, or let the liquid cool in order to pour it into an ice-cube tray to keep for convenient future use.

This is a basic stock version. To change the taste you can add, for example, fennel, juniper berries, thyme, garlic, celeriac, cloves or any vegetable and herb that takes your fancy or fits to the dish for which you are making the stock.

A little hint

Lovage, also known as love parsley, is a very useful plant that is often used as a component in soups. It is more commonly used in southern Europe. It is hard to find in supermarkets in the northern regions, but you can ask at the grocery market or in a garden center if they can help you get one. The flavour of the plant reminds you of soup seasoning. Give it a try if you can get hold of it.

Cucumber salad

4 servings

1 cucumber, roughly grated

1 garlic clove, finely grated

Salt

1 tsp olive oil

1 tsp corn oil

Parsley or chives, finely chopped

175g single cream

Pepper

Peel the cucumber and cut it in lengthwise in half so that the seeds are exposed. With a tablespoon, spoon the core with the seeds out then roughly grate the rest of the cucumber. Put the grated cucumber in a mesh strainer or any other suitable type of sieve on top of a bowl to catch cucumber juices. Add about ¼ teaspoon of salt to the cucumber and leave to rest for five to ten minutes. Then press as much juice out of the remaining cucumber as possible.

Add the oil, the cream, the fresh herb(s) and pepper. Mix well and serve.

Those who need to avoid lactose can omit the cream, or try out a lactose-free product.

Crispy oven chicken thighs on a mixed herb salad bed

4 servings

For the chicken thighs:

8 chicken thighs, boned

Marinade:

Olive oil

Zest & juice of 1 lemon (optional)

Sprig of rosemary or tarragon, chopped

Salt and freshly ground pepper

For the salad bed:

250g choice of green salad

150g yoghurt

50g soured cream

1 clove garlic, crushed (optional)

4 tbsp olive oil

Salt and freshly ground pepper

Pre-heat the oven to 180 C. For the marinade, chop your herb of choice and put it in a shallow bowl together with the oil, lemon zest and juice and seasoning. You need enough to coat the chicken. Slash the skin of the chicken thighs diagonally two to three times, so the marinade can penetrate the chicken. Then turn them in the marinade, cover and leave in the refrigerator for between 10 minutes and an hour. Theoretically you can cook them right away, but leaving them in the marinade makes them even tastier. Cook in the oven in a roasting tin at 180 C for around 40-45 minutes or until browned and crisp around the edges.

To make the dressing, combine the yoghurt, soured cream, garlic, olive oil and mix well. Add seasoning to your liking.

Pour the dressing over the salad and toss. Place the salad on a serving plate. Cut the chicken thighs into slices and arrange them on top of the salad, and serve immediately.

Instead of packaged salad you can create your own version with the likes of romaine salad, green leaf lettuce, lollo rosso, watercress or whatever else you may like, with a mixture of herbs you prefer, such as coriander leaves, parsley, mint, and basil. You can also take your inspiration by looking at the packs and re-creating the ingredient mixtures. Salad leaves that have been cut and left in bags unfortunately change in their chemical setup quite quickly, which is recognisable from the funny smell you get when you first open some of them.

Broccoli, red pepper and rocket salad with fried eggs

4 generous servings

Olive oil

400g purple sprouting broccoli

400g red and yellow bell pepper, chopped

200g rocket, washed

Handful fresh basil leaves, cut into strips

2-3 tbsp lemon juice

4 eggs

Salt and freshly ground pepper

If you can't obtain purple sprouting broccoli you can use the florets of a normal broccoli instead.

In a pan of boiling salted water blanch the broccoli for 3 minutes, drain well and tip into iced water. Drain again and put them to the side.

Place the rocket, peppers, olive oil, lemon juice into a salad bowl and toss them to mix well. Add the broccoli and toss again.

Heat a little olive oil in a non-stick frying pan and crack the eggs into the pan. Fry them until cooked, and the egg white starts to slightly brown on the edges.

To assemble the salad, place a portion of salad on each serving plate. Place a fried egg on top and sprinkle with a little basil.

Main course

Chicken fricassée

4 servings

600 g chicken breast
2 onions, chopped into large chunks
4 carrots, peeled and chop into 1 cm chunks
2-3 stems celery, chopped into 1 cm chunks
Generous handful of parsley, as is, with stems
2 cloves
2 bay leaves
Salt
For the sauce:
60g butter
60g flour or rice flour
Up to 800 ml chicken stock
300g asparagus, cut into 2cm lengths
300g mushrooms, sliced
1tbsp lemon juice
4 egg yolks
5 tbsp whipping cream
Freshly ground pepper

Bring the water (2 litres) to the boil in a large saucepan. Meanwhile, wash and prepare all the vegetables for the stock and set aside.

Cut the chicken into large chunks.

Put the chicken pieces in the boiling water and bring back to the boil.

Now add the rest of the vegetables and herbs and cover. Leave to simmer for 35 – 45 minutes. Make sure that it is not cooking too rapidly, just slightly simmering.

While the stock is cooking prepare the asparagus and the mushrooms for adding to the sauce later on as follows:

In a small saucepan, bring some water to the boil. Trim the asparagus and remove the hard ends of the stalk, normally around one centimetre from the thick end. Cut the asparagus into sections of about 2cm and blanch in simmering water for around 3-5 minutes depending on thickness. To have them "al dente" you should just about be able to prick through them with a fork. Drain the asparagus well and leave to the side.

Slice the mushrooms and fry them in some butter or olive oil until they turn slightly brown. Leave them to the side with the asparagus, to add to the sauce later on.

Pour the stock through a sieve, and reserve 800 ml of the liquid for the sauce.

You can either freeze the rest of the stock or use some of it in which to cook the rice, instead of just using water and salt.

Take the chicken out of the stock, cut into bite-sized pieces and set aside to put in the sauce later on.

For the sauce, melt the butter in a pan on medium heat until it starts to foam. Stir in your flour of choice. Using rice flour has the incredible advantage of not going lumpy like normal flour does, and it is gluten free as well – two strikes in one. Keep stirring vigorously to make sure it does not burn. Once it starts turning into a pale yellow gooey mixture, add some stock little by little and keep on stirring energetically, using a whisk, until it thickens. Bring the sauce to the boil and simmer uncovered for about 5 minutes, stirring regularly. If the sauce thickens too much, pour in more stock and stir again until it turns back to the consistency you want. Making this sauce may need some practice, but once you've got the hang of it, it is really easy and a lot of fun.

Once the sauce is ready, add the chicken, the asparagus and the mushrooms, bring back to the boil and add a tablespoon or more of lemon juice to taste.

Whisk the egg yolks together with the whipping cream and fold the mixture into the fricassee. Leave to bubble very gently for another 2-3 minutes, but don't boil the sauce any further as otherwise some components may separate. Season with salt (if more is necessary), ground pepper and lemon juice.

This recipe goes very well with rice which can be boiled in some of that lovely leftover stock, or wild rice or noodles.

The recipe sounds very complicated at first, but do give it a try as you will learn some principles of making stock as well as making a sauce and blanching, which are all useful tools for future cooking.

You can find rice flour in the gluten-free sections of some supermarkets, or at some health food shops, some of whom will surely be happy to order it for you if they don't happen to have it.

Roast chicken with lemon and sage

4 servings

1.2 – 1.5 kg oven-ready chicken, giblets removed

125g butter, softened

20 fresh sage leaves, chopped

1 clove garlic, finely chopped

2 cloves garlic, slightly crushed

1/2 lemon, zest and juice

Salt and freshly ground pepper

Pre-heat the oven to 180 C (fan oven) or 200 C Mix together the softened butter with the finely chopped sage, chopped garlic and the lemon zest and 1 tbsp lemon juice and season with pepper. Season the chicken with salt and freshly ground pepper outside and also inside the cavity. Now loosen the skin from the flesh by gently running your fingers from the cavity side to the back of the neck, which will create a pocket for your lemon and sage butter. Also try to loosen the skin from the legs. Be careful not to pierce the skin with your nails or rip it by trying to reach in. Now take half of the lemon and sage butter and spread it inside the pockets you have just created, also around the legs. Once you have got the butter in the right places massage it in as much as you can from the outside to spread it as much as possible. Then take a little more of lemon and sage mix and smear it all over the outer skin. Whatever is left goes inside the cavity, as well as the two crushed garlic cloves, and the leftover lemon peel. Close the cavity with the skin and pin it down to stay in place with some wooden cocktail sticks (you can also tie the legs together tightly with an oven-proof string). This helps keep the moisture in.

Place the chicken in an oven dish and cook it in the oven for 1 hour and 20 minutes to 2 hours depending on size. (General rule – 25 minutes per 500g plus 20 minutes). Every half hour baste the chicken, using a spoon or ladle, coating it with the cooking juices. The chicken is ready when the juices run clear when the bird is pierced with a skewer.

Take the chicken out of the oven, cover it with foil and let it rest for around 20 minutes. Skim off the excess fat from the juice in the bottom of the roasting dish and pour the juices into a sauce-boat or jug. Once you have served the chicken on the plates pour a little of the juice over the meat.

Old fashioned brisket of beef with potato and pumpkin mash

4 servings

Brisket is one of the cheaper cuts of beef but can be one of the most delicious if you give it plenty of cooking time. The recipe is for four servings, but with brisket 'the bigger the better' is always true and it is a really good party dish.

1 kg of rolled brisket

1 large onion, chopped

Freshly ground black pepper

A little vegetable oil

Equal quantities (in volume) of potato and pumpkin

Clove of garlic, crushed (optional)

1 tbsp rosemary, chopped

1 tbsp sage, chopped

Butter

Grind some black pepper onto a plate or board and roll the joint in it. Heat the oil in a thick-bottomed heavy pan or casserole with a firm fitting lid and roll the joint in it until sealed and a little brown. Remove the joint, put in the chopped onion, glaze, and then put the cut ends of the joint on top, sealing each in turn. Meanwhile boil water in a kettle and add to the joint, almost covering it. Turn down the heat, put on the tight lid, and simmer very, very gently for four hours or more. This can also be done in the oven, at about 140 C, turning it down to 120 if it is boiling too hard. Remove and allow to rest in a warm place while cooking the vegetables. Meanwhile take the liquid in which the meat has cooked, including onions, and reduce down to a gravy. It will thicken without help. Peel and cook the potatoes until tender. Cut pumpkin flesh into cubes and cook until fork-tender. (Don't overcook or you get mush). Mash separately, then mix together. Add a generous knob of butter and the garlic if you like. Season to taste – nutmeg is also an option. If cooked right, the brisket should fall to pieces and melt in the mouth. Serve with the vegetables and plenty of gravy.

The best brisket my mother ever ate, she tells me, was 4 kilos or more, seasoned and wrapped in layer upon layer of aluminium foil, and left deep in the embers of a big bonfire in a fire pit at the end of the night. It was still piping hot and wonderfully tender the next evening. But that was in Texas.

Lamb chops with mint-yoghurt sauce

4 servings

8 lamb chops

2 tbsp butter

5 tbsp olive oil

2 tsp dried oregano

1 tbsp Dijon mustard

1 tbsp lime, juice

Salt and freshly ground pepper

50ml vegetable stock

4 tbsp yoghurt

1 tsp lime, juice

2 tbsp fresh mint chopped

Salt

200g Basmati rice

Vegetable stock

Preheat the oven to 220C

For the mint and yoghurt sauce, combine the yoghurt, lime juice, mint, and seasoning. Mix well, and let the ingredients infuse in the refrigerator until serving.

For the marinade for the lamb chops mix together the olive oil, oregano, Dijon mustard, lime juice and season. Put the lamb chops in a large bowl and pour the mixture over them. Then rub the marinade in with your hands. Cover with foil and let them marinade for around 15-20 minutes.

For the rice, bring vegetable stock to the boil and cook the rice according to package instructions.

Heat the butter and a little olive oil in an ovenproof frying pan over a high heat. Place the marinated lamb chops in the pan and fry them for 2 minutes on each side until they are crispy brown, also on the sides. Now transfer the pan to the oven and cook for 10 minutes.

To serve, place the lamb chops on the plates, skim the excess oil in the pan off the top. Put the pan back on the stove at high heat, pour in a little of the vegetable stock, and scrape the bottom of the pan to loosen any of the good browned bits. Pour a couple of tablespoon of sauce over each lamb chop. Serve with rice, mint-yoghurt sauce and vegetables of your choice.

Oven-roast root vegetables

4 servings as main dish, 8 as side-dish

3-5 tbsp olive oil

3 medium sized potatoes, cut into large chunks

3 medium sized carrots, cut into large chunks

2 medium sized parsnips, cut into pieces around 5cm long and 1 cm thick

1 small fennel, cut into three pieces, each held together by the heart of the fennel

1 white onion, cut into chunks

1 red onion, cut into chunks

3-4 cloves garlic, un-peeled (optional)

½ lemon, cut into 4 wedges

Salt and freshly ground pepper

Pre-heat the oven to 180C.

Combine and mix all of the vegetables except the lemon in a casserole dish. Season with salt and freshly ground pepper, drizzle with olive oil and mix to make sure it is all covered in oil.

Push the fennel pieces to the bottom of the pan as they need to end up lying in the juices produced during cooking. Place the lemon wedges on top of the vegetables, skin up.

Cover and cook for approximately 1 hour. After around half an hour into cooking toss the vegetables around to cover them with liquid. This prevents the vegetables on the top layer from drying out. Be careful when handling it as the liquid is steaming hot. Push the fennel down again with a long wooden spoon, then cover and put the casserole back into the oven.

Once you can handle bread in your diet again, the juices of this dish serve as a lovely dip. In principle there are many different versions you can make of this recipe that is suitable for vegetarians too.

Fusilli alla Genovese

4 servings

350g pasta (non-wheat for those with lower threshold) fusilli, or any other shape you like

4 tbsp olive oil

Handful of fresh basil leaves, whole undamaged leaves

Handful of flat leaf parsley, roughly chopped

Handful of celery leaves, roughly chopped

Mozzarella, grated

Parmesan (optional)

1 tablespoon pine nuts or roasted sun flour seeds

100ml vegetable stock

Salt

Celery leaves can be found in the middle of a celery stalk. These are still young, tender and have a lot of flavour.

For the pasta, bring some water with a little salt to the boil and drop in the pasta of choice. Stir right away, to stop the pasta from sticking to each other. Cook according to package instructions or until just tender (al dente).

While your pasta is cooking put the basil, parsley, celery leaves, nuts or seeds of choice, mozzarella and olive oil and a pinch of salt in a blender and blend until smooth. Heat the vegetable stock, stir in a little butter, then add the herb mixture from the blender. Keep on the lowest possible heat while waiting for the pasta to get ready.

Drain the pasta, and combine with the Genovese sauce. Ready.

If you can allow yourself to do so, sprinkle a little parmesan on top.

Fish pie

4 servings

Fish-infused milk:

600g fresh fish (such as cod, haddock, halibut), skinned and all bones removed

700ml full milk

1 medium onion, roughly chopped

1 medium carrot, roughly chopped

1 stalk celery, roughly chopped

1 bay leaf

1 leaf lovage (optional)

Bunch of fresh parsley

4-6 pepper corns

topping and sauce see next page

Prepare your potato layer by bringing some water to the boil with a pinch of salt in a large pan and cook for 20 minutes, or until tender. Drain the potatoes, cover with a lid and leave to the side.

While the potatoes are cooking poach the fish as follows:

For the fish-infused milk place the filets of fish in a saucepan where you can fit them across the bottom side by side - always wash hands as well as clean surfaces after handling fish and before turning to do something else. Spread the onion, carrot, celery, bay leaf, lovage, parsley and peppercorns around the fish, and add the milk to just about cover the ingredients. On a medium heat let the milk warm up, and as soon as it starts to bubble take the saucepan off the heat. Cover with a lid. The fish will continue to cook.

Heat the oven to 200 C.

After 5 minutes, take the fish out of the milk and vegetables and place on a separate plate. Now separate the vegetables from the milk by pouring it through a sieve into a bowl. Pour about 5 tablespoons of the fish-infused milk over the drained potatoes, add the butter, pepper and a pinch of salt to taste, mash them with a potato masher, and put this to the side.

For the béchamel sauce put 50g of butter in a saucepan and let it melt slowly over a low

Potato topping:

1kg floury potatoes, peeled and chopped

1tbsp butter

Salt and freshly ground pepper

Mild grated cheese, such as mild Gouda or cheddar

Béchamel sauce:

50g butter

50g flour of choice (or rice flour)

Fish-infused milk

Salt

heat. Add the same amount of your flour of choice, turn the heat up to medium, and stir constantly with a wooden spoon until you get a smooth paste. Add your warm fish-infused milk, a couple of tablespoons at a time, and stir in vigorously with the wooden spoon. It is important to keep stirring as otherwise it will go lumpy. Repeat adding little amounts of the fish-infused milk until the paste starts to become a softer texture. Switch to a whisk and continue until it eventually turns into a creamy sauce. Now turn the heat down as low as possible and let the sauce simmer for 5 minutes. If the sauce thickens too much during this time, add another couple of tablespoons of the fish-infused milk and stir again until it becomes the desired texture.

Now you can pat yourself on your back. This was the difficult bit. Plain sailing from now on.

Take the cooked fish and remove any bones that may have been previously overseen. Carefully combine the béchamel sauce with the fish, trying not to let the fish break up and become too flaky. Place this mix in a deep oven dish. Then spread the potato mash evenly on top. Sprinkle some grated cheese on top and bake in the oven for around 20 – 25 minutes. It is ready once the top starts to brown.

Parcels of fish steamed in herb sauce with oven chips

4 servings

Preheat the oven to 210 C.

For the fish parcels:

4 x 150g-200g fish fillet (cod, halibut, salmon etc), skinned and bones removed

2 garlic cloves, crushed

4 tsp parsley, finely chopped

1 tbsp rosemary, finely chopped

Lemon zest and juice of 1/2 lemon

5 tbsp olive oil

Salt & pepper

For the oven chips:

800g large potatoes

Olive oil

Salt

Pepper (optional)

For the potato chips, cut the potatoes to around 1 by 1 cm chips (or into wedges). Blanch them in simmering water for around three minutes and drain well. Spread the pieces so that they don't touch each other on a baking tray, sprinkle with oil and distribute it with your fingers so they are all in a thin film of oil, then season well.

For the wrapped fish put the garlic, parsley, rosemary, lemon zest and juice and olive oil into a bowl and season with salt and freshly ground pepper. Mix well.

Cut 4 sheets of aluminium foil or parchment paper to at least twice the length of the fish filet. Check the fish for bones that may have been overseen and place each filet on an individual piece of foil/parchment - wash hands after handling fish. Evenly distribute the parsley and rosemary mixture on top of each fish fillet with a tablespoon. Fold the foil or parchment over each fish and seal so that the fish is wrapped in a parcel with an air pocket over it. This will keep the moisture inside and steam the fish in the juices. Put the parcels on a baking tray.

Once the oven is fully pre-heated put the fish parcels in the lower part of the oven and the potato chips in the upper part of the oven and cook for 15 to 20 minutes depending on size of filets.

Shake the potatoes and turn them half way, maybe even twice through the cooking.

Take the fish parcels out and put them aside. Wait for a couple of minutes. Open the bags from the top. Caution! Be careful with your fingers and face as there will be piping hot steam escaping at the beginning.

Lift the fish onto a plate, spoon the juice over each fillet, and serve with oven crisps and vegetables of your choice.

There are many variations you can make with fish parcels. Some are with a combination herbs such as basil, chives, rosemary or sage, and some also have vegetables such as carrots and courgettes cut into julienne strips and added on top. The best thing about it is that it is a way of cooking fish that is not messy at all in comparison to other recipes. This is just one example to start you off.

With regard to the potatoes, you can also make different variations with spices that are ok for you and herbs that can withstand higher temperatures, such as rosemary and thyme.

Desserts and Baking

Low-histamine rye and spelt bread

1 loaf	Preheat the fan oven to 160°C, or 180 C without fan.
250g spelt flour	Put all the dry ingredients (spelt flour, rye flour, cumin, salt, glucose, cream of tartar)
200g rye flour	together in a bowl and mix well. Add the soda water little by little and mix well. Add
½ - 1 tsp freshly ground cumin (with a pepper mill)	the maple syrup and beat the dough with a robust cooking spoon for 3-4 minutes in order to beat out as much carbon dioxide as possible. You can also use a mixer at very
1 tsp salt	low speed, but it is possible that the dough will stick to the equipment and start wrap-
¼ tsp glucose	ping itself around it.
15g Cream of Tartar	Put some baking paper on a baking tray. Put
1 tsp maple syrup	the dough onto the baking paper and form it into a round loaf. Use a wet knife, dipped
400ml soda water	in cold water, and lightly slice the top of the loaf cross-wise. Sprinkle some whole cumin
At least ½ l water	over the top of the dough. Place the loaf in the pre-heated oven.

Place an oven-proof dish with at least ½ l water underneath the bread. This helps to make the bread nice and crusty.

Bake the bread for 70-90 minutes. Then stick a barbecue skewer into the middle and pull it out again. If some dough is still sticking to it, then the baking process is not finished. If that is the case, then turn the heat up to 180°C and bake the bread for another 10 – 20 minutes.

Take the finished loaf out of the oven and leave to cool before slicing it.

Old-fashioned rice pudding

Can also be made with tapioca, semolina or similar grains

40g short-grain (pudding) rice	Take a fairly deep oven-proof dish and simply mix the rice, sugar and milk in it. The liquid should be at least 7 cm deep. Dot the surface with some butter flakes. Sprinkle with nutmeg or coconut, if using, to taste. Do not cover. Bake in a low oven (150 C) for about 2 hours. Eat on its own or with jam, fruit or flavouring of choice.
25g sugar	
500ml full-fat milk	
A sprinkling of nutmeg, or 1 tbsp desiccated coconut	
Butter shavings	This is the simplest of puddings and can be varied in all kinds of ways, for instance

by flavouring with vanilla. Quantities can also be varied proportionally. For those with lactose intolerance, coconut milk can be substituted, though this will not give the typical brown 'skin' that many find very tasty. That is also why you need whole milk for this, and not the less fat varieties. Make the simple version first, then use your imagination!

Simple apple cake

150g self-raising flour	Chop the apples quite fine. Rub the fat into the flour, as for pastry making, until it is like breadcrumbs. Add the apple and stir in well. Add the sugar and stir in well. Add the milk tablespoon by tablespoon until a very firm dough is formed. (If it goes sticky add a sprinkling of flour to get it back.)
75g margarine	
150g cooking apples (Bramleys), weight when peeled and cored	
75g sugar	Press into a round, lined sandwich cake tin or shape to a round on a greased baking sheet.
A little milk	

Bake in the middle of the oven at 190 C for 20 minutes then reduce the heat to 160 C for a further 25 minutes. It should be light brown on top when finished. This can also be eaten hot as a pudding with cream, yoghurt, custard or a desert sauce of your choice.

Feta cheese and mint scones

Makes about 15 scones

350g self-raising flour

1 ½ tsp baking powder

Pinch of salt

75g butter, at room temperature

4 tbsp fresh mint, roughly chopped

150g feta cheese, crumbled

1 egg

150ml milk

Preheat the oven to 220 C.

Place flour, baking powder, salt and butter in a deep bowl and mix as for pastry – either by hand, rubbing between thumb and fingertips, or by machine with a dough-making appliance - until it looks like bread-crumbs.

Add the remaining ingredients and stir or blend slowly until a soft dough forms that should come away from the sides of the bowl. (If it is sticky, add a little more flour)

Turn out onto a floured or none-stick surface and roll until 1cm thick. Cut out rounds with a 6cm cutter. Do not twist the cutter otherwise scones will not rise evenly. Place well apart on a none-stick baking tray, or on baking paper. Roll out remaining dough again and continue until it is used up (about 15 scones). Brush a little milk over the tops.

Bake for 10 – 15 minutes, until well-risen and golden brown on top.

Serve warm, with butter and an optional slice of any remaining feta cheese.

The incredibly delicious milk tart

4 generous servings

200g sweet rye biscuits, crushed

75g butter

700ml full fat milk

2-3 tbsp sugar

6-7 tbsp flour

3 eggs

Vanilla from one pod

Knob of butter (optional)

ground cinnamon (optional)

For the biscuit base, melt the butter and combine it with the finely crushed rye biscuit (best done in a blender) and then mix them together well with your hands. Put the mixture in a round baking tin (diameter approx. 27cm and 2cm high) or a dish.

Press the mixture into the dish and leave aside.

For the custard, cut the vanilla pod in half lengthwise with a sharp knife and scrape out the pod's seeds with a spoon. Combine the sugar, flour and eggs and vanilla, and beat them together with a whisk. Pour the milk into a bain marie (see below) and then add the mixture to the milk as it starts heating up. Keep stirring slowly with the whisk until the mixture thickens and gets a custard-like texture but is still runny. This may take a while depending on what kind of flour you use.

If you feel specially naughty then you can add a knob of butter once the custard is ready. This will give it an even smoother texture. Stir quickly and pour evenly over the biscuit base to cover. Sprinkle with some cinnamon if you would like this extra twist. Allow the mixture to cool.

A bain marie is a heavy pan of simmering water where you place a bowl on top to slowly heat mixtures at consistent temperatures, and also to stop substances from sticking and burning onto the bottom of a pan. Bain maries can be used for making some cheesecakes, custards, or hollandaise sauce to name a few. Milk Tart is a South African dish often served at tea-time, and the recipe was given to me by my brother's lovely girlfriend, who is a busy artist and in her free time a fantastically creative cook. This recipe is only recommendable to make if you have some time and patience. When starting to stir the custard, it may appear that nothing is happening at all, so take a Zen approach. It is a great excuse for not being able to do anything else but monotonously stir for half an hour or so. When you are in the right frame of mind it is quite calming, and the outcome is worth it.

Wholemeal melt-in-the-mouth gingerbread

100g plain flour	Sieve the plain flour, salt, cinnamon, ginger and bicarbonate of soda into a large bowl. Add the wholemeal flour and Demerara sugar and stir.
¼ tsp salt	
½ level tsp ground cinnamon	Warm the butter, golden syrup and dark treacle gently in a pan until the butter melts.
3 level tsp ground ginger	Beat the egg and stir into the milk.
1 level tsp bicarbonate of soda	Mix all the ingredients together – you should be able to pour it out of the bowl. If not, add more milk.
100g wholemeal flour	
40g Demerara (brown) sugar	Pour into a loaf tin, or a square cake tin, lined with greased greaseproof paper. Sprinkle on the flaked almonds if you choose.
100g butter	
100g golden syrup	Bake in the centre of the oven at 150 C for an hour. Test with a skewer, which should come out clean. If not, bake for up to another half hour. The cake should be firm and spring back when prodded with a finger (ouch, hot!).
100g dark treacle	
1 large egg	
150ml milk	This cake tastes even better if allowed to cool off overnight.
10g flaked almonds (optional)	

Relishes and Sauces

Parsley and onion relish

Handful of parsley, finely chopped

1 onion, sweet variety, finely chopped

Olive oil

Juice of half a lemon

Salt & pepper

In a bowl, mix the chopped parsley and onion with the oil and lemon juice. Season to taste.

This is a recipe a friend of mine talked about one evening, when the subject turned to cooking. He told us that this dish is commonly eaten in Spain as part of a main dish, on salads or as a spread.

Simple garlic sauce

150g strained yoghurt

1 clove of garlic, crushed

salt

Mix together all of the ingredients, and leave in refrigerator for around half an hour so that the flavour of the garlic has time to combine with the yoghurt.

Greek Tzatziki

150g strained yoghurt

1-3 cloves garlic, crushed

Half a cucumber

Salt

Peel the cucumber and cut it in half lengthwise so that the seeds are exposed. With a tablespoon, spoon the core with the seeds out then roughly grate the rest of the cucumber. Put the grated cucumber in a mesh strainer or any other suitable type of sieve on top of a bowl to catch cucumber juices. Add about ¼ teaspoon of salt to the cucumber and leave to rest for half an hour. Then press as much juice out of the remaining cucumber as possible. This makes the Tzatziki less moist in the end. In a fresh bowl mix together the cucumber pulp with the yoghurt and garlic. Ready to eat!

Some people may like to add a little lemon juice, fresh dill, parsley, mint, basil leaves, pepper or olive oil or a combination of these.

Fig sauce

12 figs

3 tbsp sugar

235ml water

1 tbsp butter

1 tbsp cornstarch or rice flour

2 tbsp lemon juice

Scrape the flesh out of the figs with a tea-spoon. Combine the flesh of the figs, sugar, water and butter in a saucepan. Bring to a boil, and simmer around 5 minutes or just until figs are tender.

Add the corn-starch and lemon juice, mixing until smooth and also add this to the fig mixture while stirring. Continue to cook over a low heat and continue stirring until it thickens and is bubbling.

This sauce goes well with ice cream and pancakes.

Skordalia

250g floury potatoes, peeled

2 medium garlic cloves, crushed

7 tbsp olive oil

1 tbsp lemon juice

Salt

Peel and boil the potatoes until cooked. Once cooked let the potatoes cool off to room temperature, or at least so they are no longer very hot, and mash.

Meanwhile, peel and crush, or preferably mash, the garlic cloves. Mix the garlic together with all the olive oil and some salt in a blender. Then add the potato mash and blend at low speed until it becomes creamy. Add lemon juice at the very end, giving it one more quick stir. Let the Skordalia cool down.

This dish can be served as a starter, or on the side of any meat dish as well as Mediterranean vegetable dishes. It has been one of my favourites for years. It is best eaten when cold.

Pestos

30g sunflower seeds, or pine nuts or pumpkin seeds

A generous handful of fresh herbs, such as fresh basil, coriander, flat leaf parsley, rocket, celery leaves

Olive oil

1-2 cloves garlic, peeled and roughly chopped

Lemon juice - optional

Salt

Lightly brown the seeds or pine nuts in a small frying pan on medium heat. Be careful not have the heat too high as they tend to burn easily. Take the seeds/nuts off the heat when light brown and put them in a cool bowl as they will continue to cook for a little longer. Let them cool.

Meanwhile wash your choice of herbs and roughly chop them before you put them in the blender. Add the roughly chopped garlic, seeds/nuts, salt and freshly ground pepper. While blending, add olive oil little by little until it becomes a paste-like consistency.

Basil is normally used as the main component in green pestos in combination with other herbs. The classic Pesto Genovese is made of Genovese basil, pine nuts, garlic, olive oil and salt.

To add red colour and extra vitamins you can add de-seeded, grilled, and skinned red bell peppers.

You can use pesto on many different dishes, for example as part of a potato salad where you can add some lemon to give it acidity if you like, with a green mixed salad adding more olive oil to help it cover the leaves, or with any type of noodles. You can also spread it on savoury biscuits as a snack in between.

Mint sauce

1 handful of fresh mint leaves, chopped

1 tbsp lemon juice

1-2 tbsp apple juice

1 tbsp sugar or caster sugar

Mix all the ingredients in a bowl and let them rest in the refrigerator for half an hour.

23.   The Food Diary

Food Diary Instructions

Writing a food diary should assist you, your doctor and the dietician with the following:

Finding the cause of your symptoms

Tracking your reactions

Making the necessary changes to your diet

Try to insert as much information as you can. The more you write in, the higher the likelihood that you can get to the bottom of it all. Here are some instructions for what you should include in your diary.

Week beginning: Insert the start date of the week.

Time: Insert the time when you had the food and/or drink.

Food & drink (incl. approx. amounts): Record what food you ate, preferably with approximate amounts eg. in ml, pints, cups, grams, tsp, tbsp, or if you can't measure them, for example in a restaurant, describe the amount eg. 1 glass, a handful, number of items of a certain food.

Time of reaction: Insert the time when your reaction started and how long it persisted.

Description of symptoms: Describe what happened, how it came about, e.g. rumbling in upper abdomen followed by diarrhoea, or light patch that turned into an itchy, painful bump around the lips.

Severity (1-10): Note how bad or painful the symptoms were on a scale from 1-10, also compared to earlier reactions.

Medicine (incl. daily amounts): Record any medication or supplements, the brand and strength of tablets (found on package information), how many and time taken.

Important conclusions reached during this week /notes: Write down any thoughts on your progress or worsening of the condition in that week. Make notes about anything else that may trouble you. You may have had more stress that week. For example, you may have realised that a certain food item has been eaten more frequently and that symptoms seem to be turning up soon after you ate it. Ask your doctor /dietician what else they suggest you should record here.

Download the food diary for free here:

www.histamineintolerance.org.uk/food-diary

24.   SOURCES & FURTHER READING

Books

Histamin-Intoleranz, Histamin und Seekrankheit, Reinhart Jarisch, Thieme Verlag

Histamin-Intoleranz, Endlich Schluss mit den Beschwerden, Thilo Schleip, Trias Verlag

Wegweiser Nahrungsmittelintoleranzen, Univ. –Doz. Dr. med Maximilian Ledochowski, Trias Verlag

Histaminarm kochen und sich wohl fühlen, Histaminarm Kochen, Verband d. Dipl. Diätassistentinnen & EMB Österreichs, Krenn Verlag

Nahrungsmittelunverträglichkeit (Histamin Intoleranz), Dr.Grace M.D.Abbot; Dr. Camille Lieners; Dr. Isabella Mayer; Dr. Albert Missbichler; Dr. Markus Pfisterer; Mag. Helmut Schmutz, Verlag: HSC 3001 Mauerbach; Auflage: 1.(2006)

The desk encyclopedia to microbiology by Moselio Schaechter, Joshua Lederberg,Pg 496/497

Oxford Medical Dictionary

Scientific papers

Histamine and histamine intolerance, Laura Maintz, Natalija Novak (2007), The American journal of clinical nutrition 85 (5) p. 1185-96

Die verschiedenen Gesichter der Histaminintoleranz, Konsequenzen für die Praxis, Laura Maintz, Thomas Bieber and Natlija Novak, Deutsches Ärzteblatt 2006; 103(51–52):A 3477–83.

Effects of histamine and diamine oxidase activities on pregnancy: a critical review. Laura Maintz, Verena Schwarzer, Thomas Bieber, Katrin van der Ven, Natalija Novak Human reproduction update 14 (5) p. 485-95

Histamine-free diet: treatment of choice for histamine-induced food intolerance and supporting treatment for chronic headaches. F Wantke, M Götz, R Jarisch (1993)

Clinical and experimental allergy : journal of the British Society for Allergy and Clinical Immunology 23 (12) p. 982-5

Joneja JMV and Carmona Silva C. Outcome of a histamine-restricted diet based on chart audit. Journal of Nutritional and Environmental Medicine 2001;11(4):249-262

Wine and headache.R Jarisch, F Wantke (1996), International archives of allergy and immunology 110 (1) p. 7-12

Alcohol-histamine interactions, S M Zimatkin, O V Anichtchik, Alcohol and alcoholism (Oxford, Oxfordshire) 34 (2) p. 141-7

Wirkung, Permeation und Katabolismus von Histamin an isolierten Dickdarmepithelien des Schweins, Frank Ahrens, Dissertation 2003

Diamine oxidase(DAO)enzyme and gene. SchwelbergerHG. In: Falus A, ed. Histamine: biology and medical aspects. Budapest, Hungary: SpringMed Publishing, 2004:43–52.

Analysis of diamine oxidase gene polymorphisms in patients with inflammatory bowel disease, J. Petersen, H. G. Schwelberger M. Raithel (2001), Inflammation Research 50 p. S68 - S69

Non-IgE-mediated mast cell stimulation, F L Pearce (1989), Ciba Foundation symposium 147 p. 74-87; discussion 87-92;

Histamine release during morphine and fentanyl anesthesia, C E Rosow, J Moss, D M Philbin, J J Savarese (1982), Anesthesiology 56 (2) p. 93-6

Ernährungsphysiologie, Biogene Amine und Histamin – Genuss oder Verdruss? By Dr. Missbichler. Dr Markus Pfisterer, Sciotec Diagnostic Technologies GmbH Vienna, Austria; Privatpraxis Dr. med. M. Pfisterer, Heilbronn, Germany. Ernährung aktuell 3/2007

Sibley E et al.: Genetic variation and lactose intolerance: detection methods and clinical implications. Am J Pharmacogenomics 2004;4(4):239-45. PMID 15287817

Nahrungsmittelunverträglichkeiten - Umgang mit Betroffenen im pflegerischen Alltag, Sabine Geyr Oktober 2006.

Histamine intolerance: a metabolic disease? H G Schwelberger (2010) Inflammation research : official journal of the European Histamine Research Society ... [et al.] 59 Suppl 2 p. S219-21

Review of Wireless Sensor Technologies and Applications in Agriculture and Food Industry: State of the Art and Current Trends, Sensors 2009, 9(6), 4728-4750; doi:10.3390/s90604728A

Karen du Plessis, Harris Steinman. Practical Aspects of Adverse Reactions to Peanut referencing to Fremont S, Moneret-Vautrain DA, Zitouni N, Kanny G, Nicolas JP. Histamine content in peanuts. Allergy 1999;54: 528-529

Steinhoff M. Griffiths C. Church M., Lugar TA. Histamine. In: Burns T, Breathnach S. Cox N. Griffiths C. Eds. Rook's textbook of dermatology. Oxford, United Kingdom: Blackwell Science, 2004:9.50-2

Biogene Amine – Ernährung bei Histamin-Intoleranz, pg 53/Alkoholika, Andreas Steneberger, Umwelt & Gesundheit 2/2007

Biogenic amines in foods: Histamine and food processing, S. Bodmer, C. Imark, M. Kneubühl (1999), Inflammation Research 48 (6) p. 296-300

Prof.Dr.med. Ralf Bauer, Universitätsklinikum Bonn Klinik u.Poliklinik f.Dermatologie; Substanzen die DAO negativ beeinflussen.

Random and systematic medication errors in routine clinical practice: a multicentre study of infusions, using acetylcysteine as an example; R E Ferner,1 N J Langford,1 C Anton,1 A Hutchings,2 D N Bateman,3 and P A Routledge2

Daily variations of serum diamine oxidase and the influence of H1 and H2 blockers: A critical approach to routine diamine oxidase assessment F. Wantke, D. Proud, E. Siekierski, A. Kagey-Sobotka (1998), Inflammation Research 47 (10) p. 396-400

Effect of radiographic contrast media on histamine release from human mast cells and basophils, P T Peachell, S K Morcos (1998),The British journal of radiology 71 (841) p. 24-30

Incidence and clinical importance of perioperative histamine release: randomised study of volume loading and antihistamines after induction of anaesthesia. Trial Group Mainz/Marburg, W Lorenz, D Duda, W Dick, H Sitter, A Doenicke, A Black, D Weber, H Menke, B Stinner, T Junginger (1994), Lancet 343 (8903) p. 933-40

Folkers K., Shizukuishi S., Willis R., Scudder S. L., Takemura K., Longenecker J. B. The biochemistry of vitamin B6 is basic to the cause of the Chinese restaurant syndrome. Hoppe-Seyler's Z. Physiol. Chem. 1984;365:405-414

Chin K. W., Garriga M. M., Metcalfe D. D. The histamine content of oriental foods. Food Chem. Toxicol. 1989;27:283-287

Sorbic Acid - Compound Summary (CID 23665582), NCBI - PubChem

Law

Milk and milk products regulations (Scotland), Food Standards Agency, 19 May 2003

Current EU approved additives and their E Numbers, Food Standards Agency, 26 April 2010

Government Fisheries Policy 2027, www.defra.gov.uk/foodfarm/fisheries/documents/fisheries2027vision.pdf

COMMISSION REGULATION (EC) No 2073/2005 of 15 November 2005 on microbiological criteria for foodstuffs: http://eur-lex.europa.eu/LexUriServ/site/en/oj/2005/l_338/l_33820051222en00010026.pdf

Zusatzstoffe, die zum Färben von Lebensmitteln oder zum Erzielen von Farbeffekten bei Lebensmitteln zugelassen sind, Anlage 1 (zu § 3 Abs. 1 und § 7), Lebensmittel- und Futtermittelgesetzbuch, Bundesrepublick Deutschland.

Verordnung über die Zulassung von Zusatzstoffen zu Lebensmitteln zutechnologischen Zwecken (Zusatzstoff-Zulassungsverordnung - ZZulV); Ausfertigungsdatum: 29.01.1998, Bundesministeriums der Justiz in Zusammenarbeit mit der juris GmbH

Correspondence

Correspondence with Department of Health, Customer Service, E-Mail Response to your Query : - Ref:DE00000413177 - Test for Histamine Intolerance, 09.06.2009

Articles

Which? Magazine, The truth about allergy testing, August 2008 Edition.

Bauchweh nach Spaghetti Bolognese, Christina Maria Hack, 20 September 2003, Die Presse

PharmCare, Fortbildungsartikel 01/2008, Laktoseintoleranz, Fruktoseintoleranz, Fruktosemalabsorption.

Welt online, Holger Kroker, Sensoren wachen über lückenlose Kühlkette, 25.11.2005;

Picnic Season: Happy Food Poisoning. The Why? Files, 16. August 2007;

Ein Polymer-Sensor soll künftig vor verdorbenem Fisch warnen, Deutscher Presse Pool, August 2007;

University chemists developing 'dipstick' test that could reduce risk of food poisoning, South Carolina University, USC News, 23. March 2007

Teasing Apart Chemicals, Scientists Unlock One More of Sleep's Secrets, by ANAHAD O'CONNOR, The New York Times Health Supplement, June 15, 2004

Burger bars replace NHS coffee shops, Trusts to ditch volunteers for fast-food income, Jo Revill, Health Editor, Guardian/The Observer, 28 May 2006

Costa coffee colonises the NHS, The Independent, 04 November 2008

Other

Fakten über Mononatriumglutamat, Food Today 11/2002, EUFIC - Europäisches Informationszentrum für Lebensmittel

Food Standards Agency UK, Independent Government Agency to protect public health

Patienteninformation Lactose-Intoleranz, Klinik Universität Mainz,

Prim. Doz. DDr. Hans Schön, Institutsletter: Lactoseintoleranz, Milchzuckerunverträglichkeit, Dr. Schön – Zöliakie – Praktische Tipps Institutsletter, Ausgabe 20/06

Patienteninformation, Histaminunverträglichkeit - Histaminintoleranz, Facharztpraxis Labor Doz. Schön

Patient information leaflet, acetylcysteine for prevention of kidney damage, UHSM Foundation Trust, review April 2009

Websites

food intolerance network - www.food-intolerance-network.com

NMI Portal - www.nahrungsmittel-intoleranz.com

Allergy UK - www.allergyuk.org

Coeliac UK - www.coeliac.org.uk/coeliac_disease

University of Iowa – Dietary Fructose Intolerance - www.uihealthcare.com/topics/medicaldepartments/foodandnutrition/dfi/index.html

Foodsmatter.com - http://www.foodsmatter.com

Leben mit Lactoseintoleranz, Verein der Laktoseintoleranz - www.vli-ev.de

www.laktobase.at, Regelschmerzen durch Histamin; September 2008, Forum

LI, HIT und FI – Forum, Histaminintoleranz => Allgemeine INFO & Diskussionen

Food Standards Agency - www.eatwell.gov.uk

Keeping food safe – cleaning, Food Standards Agency

Healthy diet – Hygiene Standards, Food Standards Agency

Healthy diet – Fruit & veg, Food Standards Agency

Healthy diet – Starchy foods, Food Standards Agency

Health issues – Fish allergy, Food Standards Agency

Notes from a hospital bed, the ramblings of a poor sod forced to spend months in traction in an NHS hospital - www.blogcatalog.com/blog/welcome-to-wallyworld/a46e93e40d6c0733fdac1e6bd43c7c5c

Initiative of Wageningen University, Netherlands - www.food-info.net, alphabetical list of E-numbers

SPECIAL THANKS to

Food Scientist and Researcher Ronke Shona in London!